Published in the United States of America

This Bramcost Publications edition is an unabridged republication
of the rare original work first published in 1953.

www.BramcostPublications.com

ISBN 10: 1-936049-55-4
ISBN 13: 978-1-936049-55-4

Library of Congress Control Number: 2011924226

Bramcost
Publications

# how to

# MAKE APRONS

## Vintage Patterns for Making Home, Garden, Utility & Craft Aprons

by ROXA WRIGHT

*assisted by Margot Knox*

*sketches by Catherine Karuschkat*

**CONTENTS**

# Foreword

Aprons today are indeed the heirs of all the ages. The varieties in this book are but a sampling of possibilities. On the whole they have been selected for use, although a few decorative ones are also included.

Historically, aprons have been much more than a utilitarian adjunct to dress. The gods of ancient Crete are depicted wearing them, so too, the Pharaohs of Egypt and their subjects, both men and women. Roman legionaries used aprons made of strips of leather as protection in battle and today the apron is an important symbol in Masonic rites.

Long white aprons of great elegance, finely pleated and adorned with lace, drawnwork and embroidery appear in Flemish and German paintings, and those of Marie Antoinette were legendary. Playing milkmaid at the Petit Trianon, she often wore a wide-ruffled white muslin apron, and she started a vogue for aprons of fine silk, even of gold lace.

Meanwhile the butchers, the bakers, and the cobblers of the world, farmers' wives, nursemaids, and seamstresses, all developed aprons suited to their needs and wore them with pride as a badge of office. Such aprons offer us a wonderful diversity of inspiration in design and fabric. Whether you cook, sew, wash babies or dogs, garden on your knees, gather flowers in your skirt, or wear aprons only decoratively and just for fun, I hope you will find here a type designed just for your particular need.

Roxa Wright

# How to Use a Graph Pattern

The patterns and designs shown are overlaid with lines forming squares. Regardless of the size of the square shown, each square represents one square inch, unless otherwise noted.

To enlarge a pattern to true size, you will need a piece of paper as long and as wide as the number of inches represented by the graph. The paper should have perfectly square corners. If the outline is simple, as the shape of an apron, mark off and number inches along the edges of the paper just as they are on the graph. Then, to find where design lines begin and end, start at upper corner and count down and across the number of inches represented by squares on the graph pattern. Draw in straight lines with a yardstick. Draw curves by locating several points on each and joining them with a connecting line.

For more intricate graphs, as an embroidery design, rule your paper off in one-inch squares. Then, forgetting the many squares, draw in just one square at a time, exactly what's shown in the corresponding square on the small drawing of the design you wish to use. Keep the relation of your lines to the side lines of the square the same as those in the small drawing. For instance, if the design in the small drawing crosses the top line of the little square at a point one-third of the way from the right, then it should do the same thing in your large drawing. If the line crosses the side line at a point almost in the corner, it should do so in the enlargement. The line connecting these points will be curved or straight according to what it is on the small drawing, and should look exactly like it, only larger. By considering each small square by itself and making a large square just like it, you will find that you can make the pattern with no difficulty.

Our patterns are marked just like commercial tissue patterns except that dots are used instead of perforations. Three dots in a triangle mean to lay pattern on a fold. Some of the graphs shown are only pattern-diagrams; others are cutting layouts also.

## Group Sewing for Bazaars

Bazaar committees often sew in groups. Factory methods, adapted to their use, step up production and result in garments of a more uniformly high quality.

**PATTERNS**

Patterns to be used often, should be of heavy paper and not folded. Write on each piece (1) the name of model, (2) size, and (3) the name of section, as "bib" or "side gore." Perforate one corner of each piece and string pieces together on twine, each size by itself. Hang all sizes of one model on one nail.

**MAKING A MARKER**

A marker is a layout drawn on paper of what you intend to cut, and you cut through it along with the fabric. Usually in cutting one size of any garment, there is some waste on the cutting layout. But if the same model is to be cut of the same material in a number of sizes, you can save fabric by doing as a factory cutter does—making a marker and mixing the pieces of all the sizes where they best fit in on the layout. If twice as many of a favorite size are required, repeat it twice on the marker. Make the marker of any lightweight wrapping paper the same width as the proposed fabric. Its length is of course limited by the length of the cutting table. Always make marker for fabric spread flat, not folded.

Examine the width of all the pieces of fabric. Then make the marker the actual width of the narrowest piece. (So-called 36-inch fabric may actually vary from 35 to 37 inches.) Grouping pieces to best advantage, outline each pattern piece with pencil. Ties and belts go together with no waste. Curved pieces fit in like magic and it is generally possible to avoid piecing.

After outlining a pattern piece on the marker, always write on it the model, size, and section. As markers are made for fabric spread flat, it will be necessary to draw twice the outline of any piece of which you must cut two and to flop any piece ordinarily cut on fold, to give the entire outline.

### SPREADING FABRIC

Use marker as a guide in spreading the material, allowing a small amount for safety. Keep all selvages even on one side. Let the other side fall as it will. After as many layers as desired have been spread (12 to 15 is the limit for hand-cutting), lay the marker on top, lining it up most carefully with even edge. Pin through each pattern outline to catch fabric underneath.

### CUTTING

For multiple cutting, the best shears are of the 11- or 12-inch tailor type. If there is much cutting to be done, adhesive tape on the hand where the shears touch will serve as a protection. Always cut through marker and fabric.

### MARKING DOTS

Using an ice pick, with a smart tap of palm or hammer, push it through all layers vertically. (To protect the cutting table, place a piece of plywood under point to be marked.) This spreads threads of material without breaking them. The mark later disappears. If marks are hard to see, hold fabric to light.

### NOTCHES

In multiple cutting, make a single small cut at right angles of fabric rather than a notch.

### BUNDLING

Before pieces are taken off table, plan sewing procedure. Tie each stack of pieces together with its piece of marker with string.

### PLANNING THE SEWING

As an example, take the pinafore on page 33. Set up three machines with hemmers. (See use of hemmer page 112.) While one worker hems all ruffles, another hems belt ties, and the third joins skirts with the false French seam done on a hemmer. The bibs all go to a worker whose machine is set up for straight stitching. Another worker may be closing and turning the ends of the straps. When she has finished the operation on a bundle, the worker ties it together again with the identifying marker piece. Then the bundle is ready for the next operation.

Ruffles will now go to a worker whose machine is set up for shirring. Either the standard shirring attachment which, after a little practice, can be adjusted exactly for the job at hand, or a loose machine stitch can be used.

After seaming, skirts go to a worker who will stitch the first turn of the hems (see page 112.) They should then go to a presser, who will turn and press hems at sides and bottom. They now go to the handsewers, who put in hems, and after the hemming they go by bundles to the shirrer.

### ASSEMBLING

The ruffles, straps, and bibs, grouped by sizes, go to a worker, who assembles the tops (see page 113.) This is a relatively slow job, so it requires twice as many workers as the shirring or hemming. The assembled tops, belts, ties, and shirred skirts next go by size-bundles to the final assemblers. They attach top and ties to belt and belt to skirt. Sewing on buttons and making buttonholes may be done by hand or by machine.

## Paneled Coverall

*(Medium Size—Adjustable)*

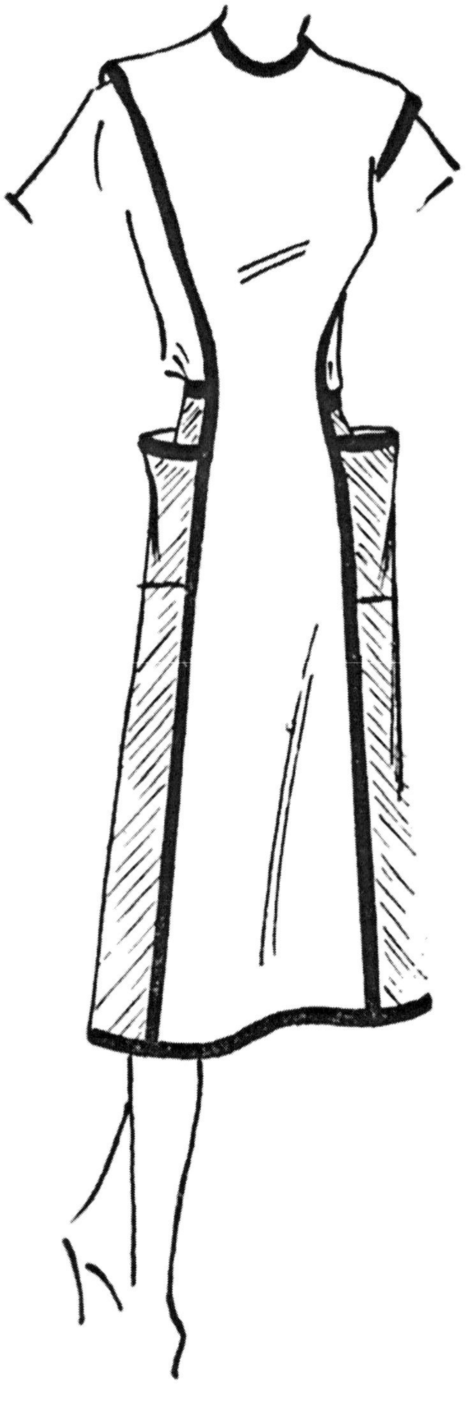

This apron may be made of two colors to give slimming lines as a bonus to its cover-up job. Ours was made of red with light blue side panels, and navy bias facings. It is entirely joined and finished with bias facing and ties at neck and waist.

**MATERIALS**

1 yard and 13 inches of one color for center panels, and 31 inches of a second color for side gores and pockets; *OR* 2 yards and 8 inches of a single color; 12 yards of extra-width bias facing.

### CUTTING

Use cutting layout on page 14. This pattern is for medium size. Add or subtract width on side gore only to alter size, as shown by dotted line, adjusting width of pockets by corresponding amount. Dotted line indicates back neck and shoulder line, solid line is for front neck and shoulder line. Slit back piece down center.

### SEWING

1. Finish tops of pockets and tops of side gores with bias facing turned toward outside and topstitched.
2. Turn in raw edges and topstitch bottoms of pockets to gores along dotted line.
3. Pin sides of pockets to sides of gores, matching notches, to be caught in later in seams.
4. Join shoulder seams in usual manner.
5. Join gores and center panels so that raw edges are turned toward the outside.
6. Stitch seams, at the same time applying bias facing so that it will turn toward center panels. Begin this seam at front hem edge, go up front, over shoulder, and down back in one continuous stitching. Topstitch the bias facing to center panels.
7. Beginning at back neck edge, face entire outside edge, including bottom edge, except neckline.
8. Make a tie 8 inches long, by doubling bias facing. Continue with the same piece of bias to face neck edge and end other side with another 8-inch tie.
9. Make 2 similar 8-inch ties and sew securely to back at waistline.

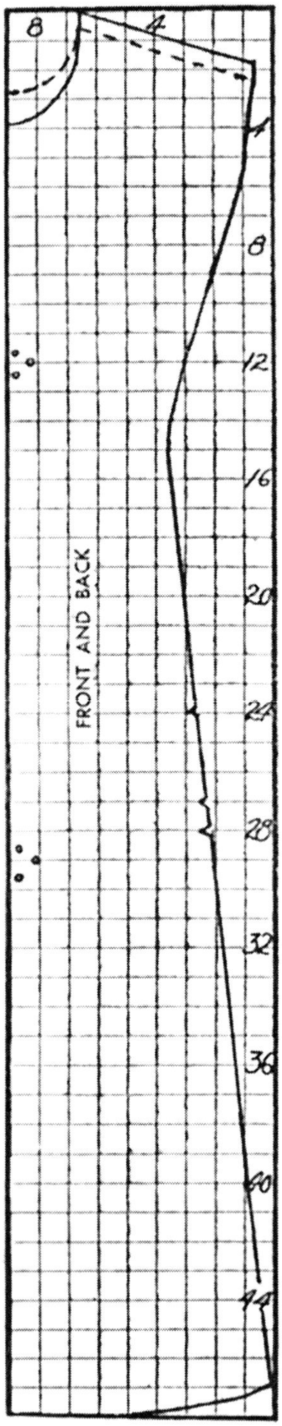


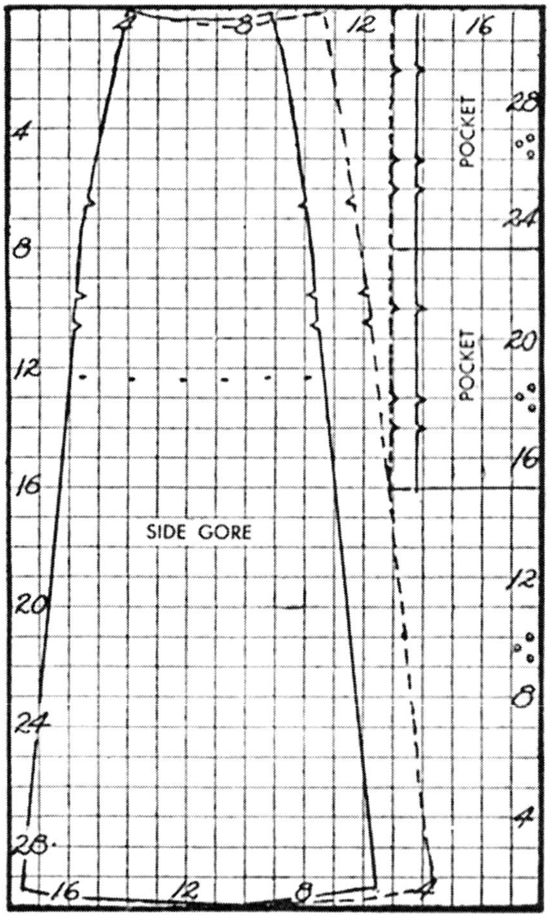


CUTTING LAYOUT

FOR

PANELED COVERALL

# Washing Apron

*(One Size—Adjustable)*

This terry-cloth apron covers you completely for any splashy job yet allows ease of movement. If it's the dog you're washing, release the buttonholes in back when you're finished, and cover him quickly with the apron to forestall his first spraying shake.

**MATERIALS**

2½ yards 36-inch terry cloth; 10 yards of extra-width bias tape; a button.

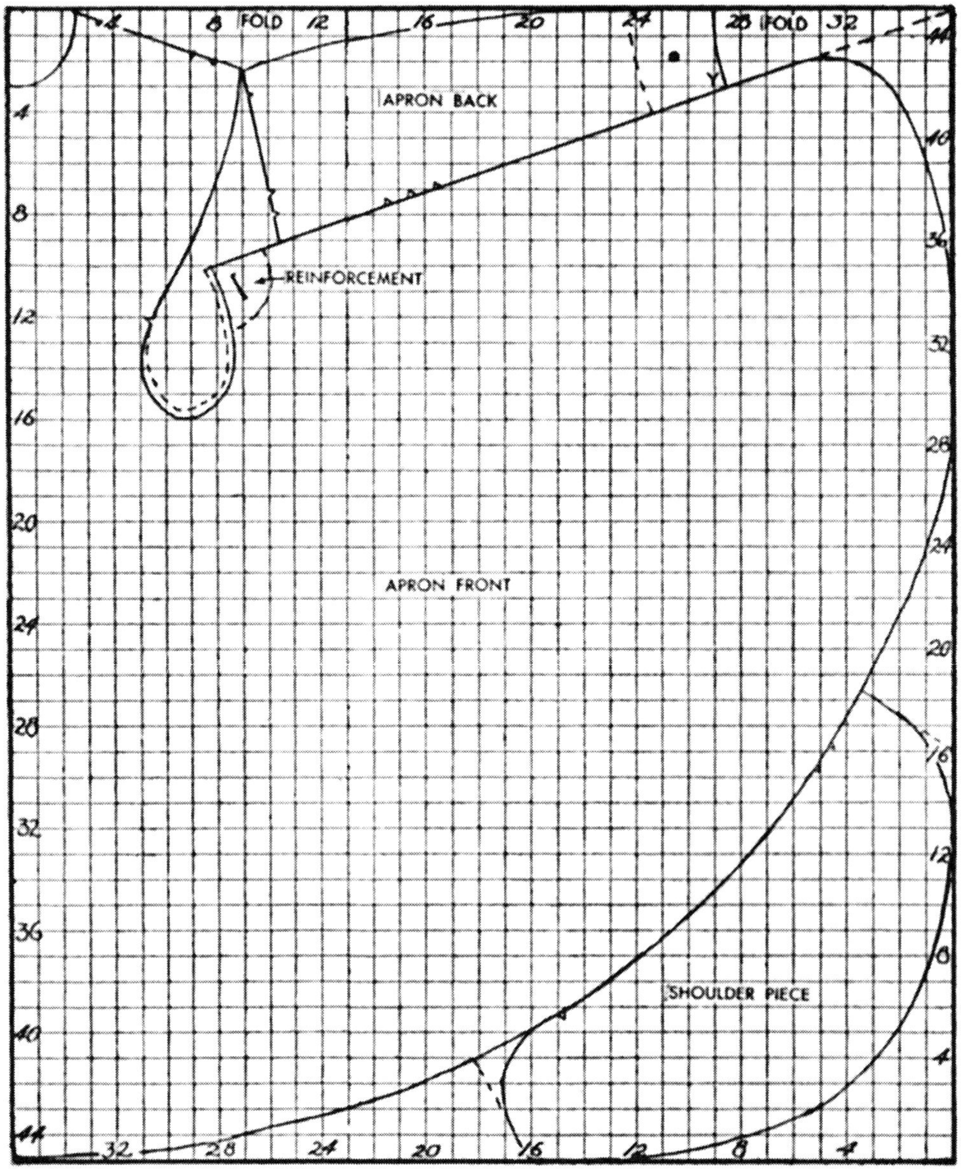


CUTTING LAYOUT FOR WASHING APRON

**CUTTING**

Follow cutting layout using fabric full width, folded crosswise. Pattern is made to fit 28-inch waistband. For smaller waistline, cut curve smaller as shown by dotted line. For larger waistline cut slightly deeper curve than shown.

**SEWING**

**Note** In seaming terry cloth, make a ⅜-inch seam, open seam and topstitch on each side ⅛ inch from seam.

1. Join center front seam, taking seam the width of selvage and topstitch on each side ⅛ inch from seam.
2. Join front and back at shoulders, matching notches.
3. Reinforce back corner with small flat facing as shown by dotted line. Do not turn in edges but stitch all around ⅛ inch from edge.
4. Join shoulder pieces to each side of apron top, matching notches.
5. Bind inside edges (except bottom ones) of back pieces and front neck edge.
6. Lap ends of back pieces so that points "Y" coincide and form a point in center back. Stitch square thus formed along lines of binding and ⅛ inch from two raw edges.
7. Bind around entire outer edge of apron.
8. Place button in center of lapped point in back and make buttonholes in two back reinforced corners. For slightly larger waistline, two buttons may be placed at corners of lapped portion.

# Smock

*(Medium Size—Adjustable)*

***For pocket design see page 118***

Button it front, as shown, or back. Sleeves are finished with elastic. Wear long or pushed up.

**MATERIALS**

3 yards of 36-inch fabric; ½ yard of ¼-inch elastic; 7 buttons; 2½ yards of rick-rack (optional).

## CUTTING

**Note.** Each square in this diagram equals 2 inches.

*In addition to the cutting layout shown,* cut one full width of fabric for back skirt, the same length as side front skirt. For smock opening in front, cut along line A-B; if a back opening is preferred, cut along line C-D; in each case continuing around circle for neck. To adjust pattern for larger or smaller sizes: place your palms together in front at shoulder level and have someone measure you from one wrist, straight around shoulders to other wrist. This pattern is made for a measurement of 60 inches wrist to wrist, and allows 4 inches for hems and ease. Subtract or add the exact amount by which you vary from 60 inches in this measurement. Smock is designed to fit 34-38 bust measure. If you wish to increase width of bust, move gussets slightly toward ends of sleeves; to decrease, move toward neck.

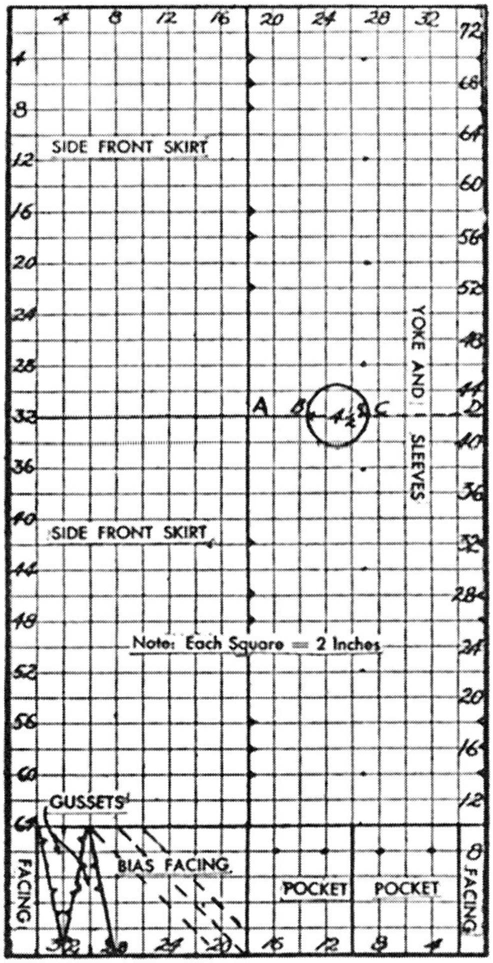

**SEWING**

1. Join underarm gussets to one side of sleeve, matching the notches and stitching to within ½ inch of each end of gusset. Clip seam allowance to end of stitching.
2. Close sleeves, matching three notches in lower sleeve and gusset notches, stitching and clipping the same as before.
3. Join fronts of skirt to back width, leaving selvage edge of fronts free.
4. Gather one long edge of skirt beginning and ending at a point 3 inches from end.
5. Join front facings to yoke opening leaving selvage edge free.
6. Join skirt to yoke, centering at back, with side seams at middle of gusset and front selvages of skirt and yoke facing even. Adjust gathers, leaving 3 inches ungathered at each side of front opening, and stitch.
7. Turn in front facing and edge of skirt and tack in place.
8. Finish neck edge with bias facing.
9. Make ½-inch casing in sleeve ends and insert elastic to fit wrist easily.
10. Make 4-inch hem in bottom edge of smock.
11. Make hems in tops of pockets, turn in raw edges, determine placement and topstitch in position.
12. On right edge of front closing, make buttonholes at top and bottom of yoke. Continue this spacing of buttonholes down the front.
13. Apply rickrack if desired, beginning at underarm and continuing around back and front edges of yoke and neck.

## Halter Top Circular Apron

*Sizes 10-12—Adjustable)*

Wear this as an apron, a beach dress, or a jumper. Omit the top for a circular, wrap around apron.

**MATERIALS**

4 yards of 36-inch fabric for sizes 10-12 and 14-16. 4¼ yards of 36-inch fabric for size 18-20. 2 yards of bias facing for all sizes; 2 buttons.

**CUTTING**

**Note.** This is not a cutting layout.

Make pattern as shown in pattern diagram. Pattern for back of skirt is shown by solid line, front of skirt by dotted line.

*In addition to pieces shown: For size 10-12,* cut waistband 4¾ inches wide and 36½ inches long. *For size 14-16,* add ½ inch to both front and back of skirt at side seam. Add ⅜ inch to all edges of halter top and move darts toward edge to correspond. Cut waistband 4¾ inches wide and 38½ inches long. *For size 18-20,* add 1 inch to both front and back of skirt at side seam. Add ¾ inch to all edges of halter top and move darts to correspond. Cut waistband 4¾ inches wide and 40½ inches long.

**SEWING**

1. Join halter pieces at center back of neck. Hem neck edge, as shown by dots. Make darts at waist and underarm.
2. Lap right halter piece over left piece so that edge meets line of dart and baste. Face outer edge of halter with bias.
3. Center halter on waistband and join as shown on page 113.
4. Try on halter, make pleat 4 inches long across back of neck to fit smoothly and stitch in place.
5. Hem tops of pockets, turn in remaining raw edges ¼ inch all around, place as shown by dots on front skirt diagram and topstitch.
6. Join skirt at center front and sides, turning in and hemming back edges as shown by dots.
7. Center skirt on back edge of waistband with wrong side of skirt facing right side of band. Stitch.
8. Turn in remaining raw edges of waistband and close, topstitching lower edge and ends.
9. Try on apron and lap right side over left in back. Mark for buttons on left side and buttonholes on right side at ends of lap-over. Make buttonholes lengthwise of waistband.
10. Hem skirt to desired length.

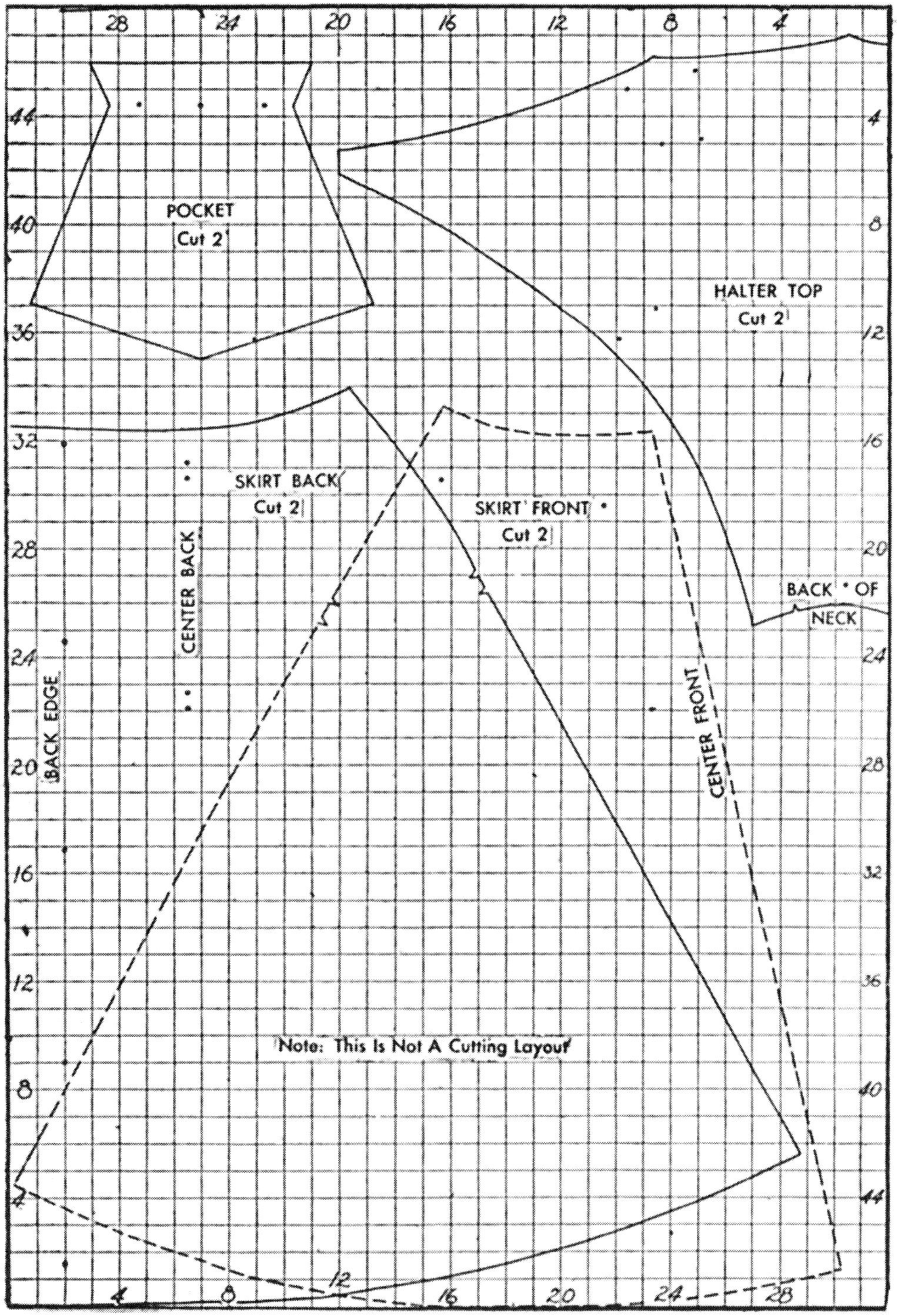

POCKET
Cut 2
HALTER TOP
Cut 2
SKIRT BACK
Cut 2
SKIRT FRONT
Cut 2
CENTER BACK
BACK EDGE
CENTER FRONT
BACK OF NECK
Note: This Is Not A Cutting Layout
28
24
20
16
12
8
4
44
40
36
32

# Maternity Coverall

(*One Size*)

Here is a comfortable apron with buttons all the way down the back and a draw-string waist.

**MATERIALS**

3 yards of 36-inch fabric with no up or down *OR* 2¾ yards of fabric and ⅜ yard contrast for facings, pocket, casing, and draw-string; buttons.

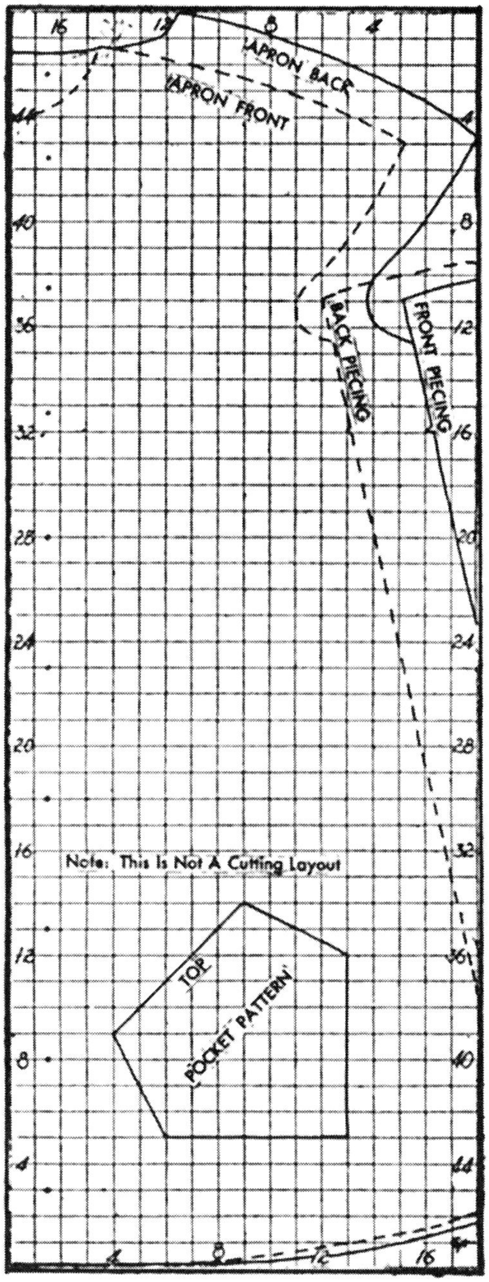


**CUTTING**

**Note.** This is not a cutting layout.

Front pattern and back skirt piecings are shown by dotted lines; back pattern and front skirt piecings by solid lines. Cut the front on center fold with back piecings fitted in beside as shown on diagram. Lay center back on selvage with front piecings fitted in beside it. From the remaining 12 inches or the contrasting fabric, cut 4 yards of 2-inch bias for casing and drawstring. Cut 2 yards of 1¼-inch bias for neck and sleeve facings. Cut pocket from the remaining triangle.

**SEWING**

1. Join piecings to lower sides of front and back skirt.
2. Seam shoulder seams and side seams.
3. Turn in back edge as shown by dots, then tack.
4. Join 1½-inch bias strips end to end and face neck and armholes.
5. Try on apron and tie tape or string around waistline. Mark position of string at front, sides, back and midpoints with pins to determine placement of casing.
6. Join 2-inch bias strips end to end.
7. Center 2-inch bias on pins marking position of casing. Turn in ¼ inch, top and bottom, and topstitch. Stop casing 1½ inches from back edge on each side. Turn in end and hem, leaving open for drawstring. Position of casing may be adjusted later, lowering or raising it as becomes necessary.
8. Fold remaining 2-inch bias in half lengthwise, stitch and turn to form drawstring. (See page 113.)
9. Thread drawstring through casing, center it and secure with a few stitches at center front to prevent it being accidentally pulled out.
10. Face top of pocket, determine placement, turn in edges ¼ inch, and topstitch.
11. Hem to desired length, leaving enough material in front hem so that it may be adjusted later as necessary.

# Wrap-Around Surplice Apron

*(Medium Size—Adjustable)*

Worn with a blouse, this apron makes a trim house dress.

**MATERIALS**

3½ yards of 36-inch fabric; 2½ yards of bias facing.

**CUTTING**

Use cutting layout shown for top, cutting on double fabric. Shoulder piece may be lengthened or shortened as desired. Remaining fabric is used crosswise for skirt.

**SEWING**

1. Hem straight edges of shoulder pieces with 1½-inch hem. Face curved edges with bias facing.
2. Lap hemmed edge of right shoulder piece over left shoulder piece and baste with raw edges even. This is front of top.
3. Join two pieces of waistband, end to end, stitching closed for 1¼ inches, leaving 1 inch opening, stitching closed 1½ inches, leaving another 1 inch opening and stitch remaining 1¼ inches. This forms slot in belt which falls at left underarm.

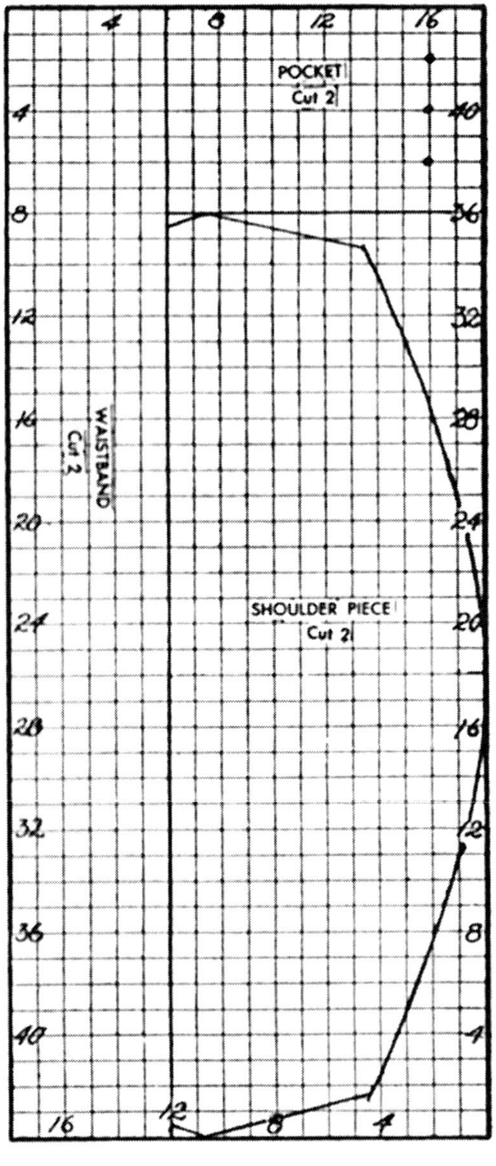

4. Measure point 7 inches (or to desired center front for your size), to right of this joining. Center front top of apron on waistband and attach in manner shown on page 113.
5. Leaving 6 inches (or desired distance for your size), measured from each outside edge of front for underarms, attach back pieces to waistband in same manner.
6. Make small hems in short edges of skirt piece.
7. Try on top of apron, pulling right end of belt through slot in side joining at left underarm. Mark with a pin the corresponding point on waistband at right underarm. Wrap left end of belt around waist and tie to right end. With a pin mark point 1 inch back from knot.
8. Gather long edge of skirt piece to fit exactly between pins placed in waistband (see Step 7). Arrange gathers so that portion of skirt falling underneath at front when skirt is tied, is flat for a space of 12 inches, the rest gathered evenly.
9. Attach skirt to back edge of waistband with wrong side of skirt facing right side of waistband.
10. Close waistband and ties, turning in all raw edges and topstitching.
11. Whip together edges of slot in belt joining.
12. Hem skirt to desired length.
13. Hem top of pockets, determine placement, turn under raw edges, and top stitch in place.

## Pinafore with Shaped Bib

*(Medium Size)*

Front terminates in short yoke, buttoning in back. Full size detail of appliqué is on page 120.

**MATERIALS**

2¾ yards of 36-inch fabric; 2½ yards of bias facing. Scraps for appliqué; six strand embroidery floss; 2 buttons.

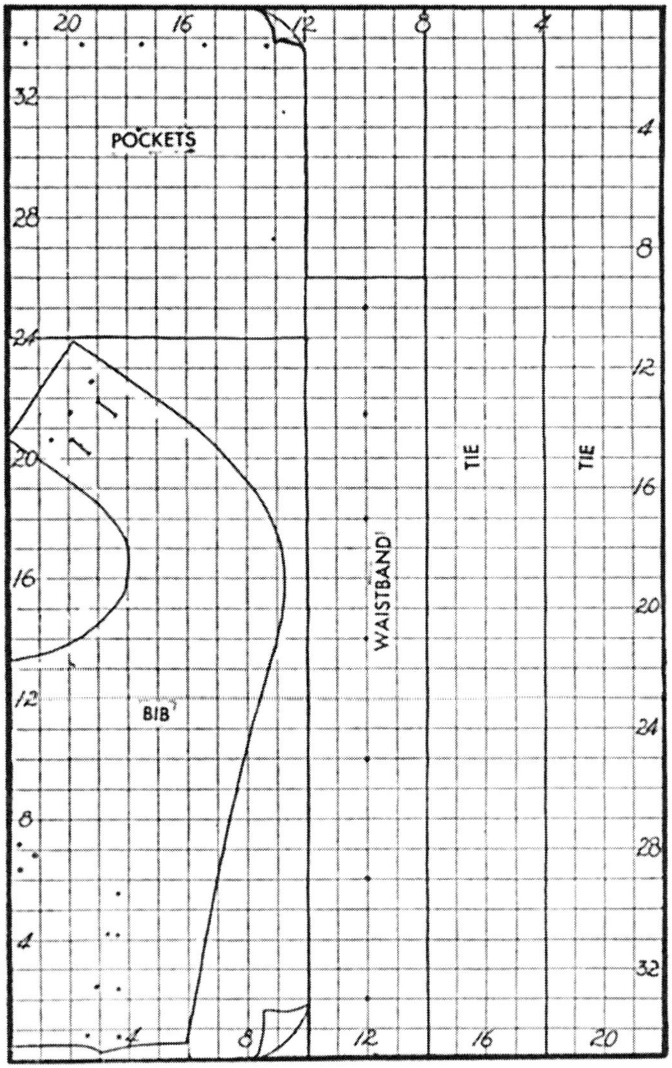


**CUTTING**

*In addition to cutting layout shown,* cut two full widths of fabric 32 inches long for apron skirt. Split one length down the center for apron side pieces. The other length is the front piece. Length of waistband may be varied if desired.

SEWING

1. Hem back edges of yoke, folding on dotted lines.
2. Stitch darts.
3. Finish sides and neck edges of yoke with bias facing.
4. Center yoke on waistband and attach as shown on page 113.
5. Join side pieces of apron skirt to front piece. Make small hems on the two back edges.
6. Gather top of skirt.
7. Center and stitch skirt on back edge of waistband with wrong side of skirt facing right side of band and draw up shirring to fit ¼ inch inside either end of band.
8. Hem ties with small hem on either side, and a 1-inch hem on one end of each.
9. Close waistband, turning raw edges and pleating and inserting raw ends of ties in ends of band.
10. Hem tops of pockets, determine placement, turn raw edges under, and topstitch in place.
11. Make two buttonholes as shown by short lines on right side of yoke back, and sew buttons on left side to match.
12. Hem skirt with a 4-inch hem, or to desired length.

# Mother-and-Daughter Pinafores or Nurse's Apron

*(Children's Sizes 2 to 12: Women's Sizes Small, Medium, and Large)*

Straps cross in back and button to waistband. This basic pattern can be varied with appliqué, lace, embroidery, pockets, or any number of different trimmings. Without ruffles it becomes a standard nurse's apron. A doll dressed in matching pinafore and peeping from a pocket, will delight any little girl.

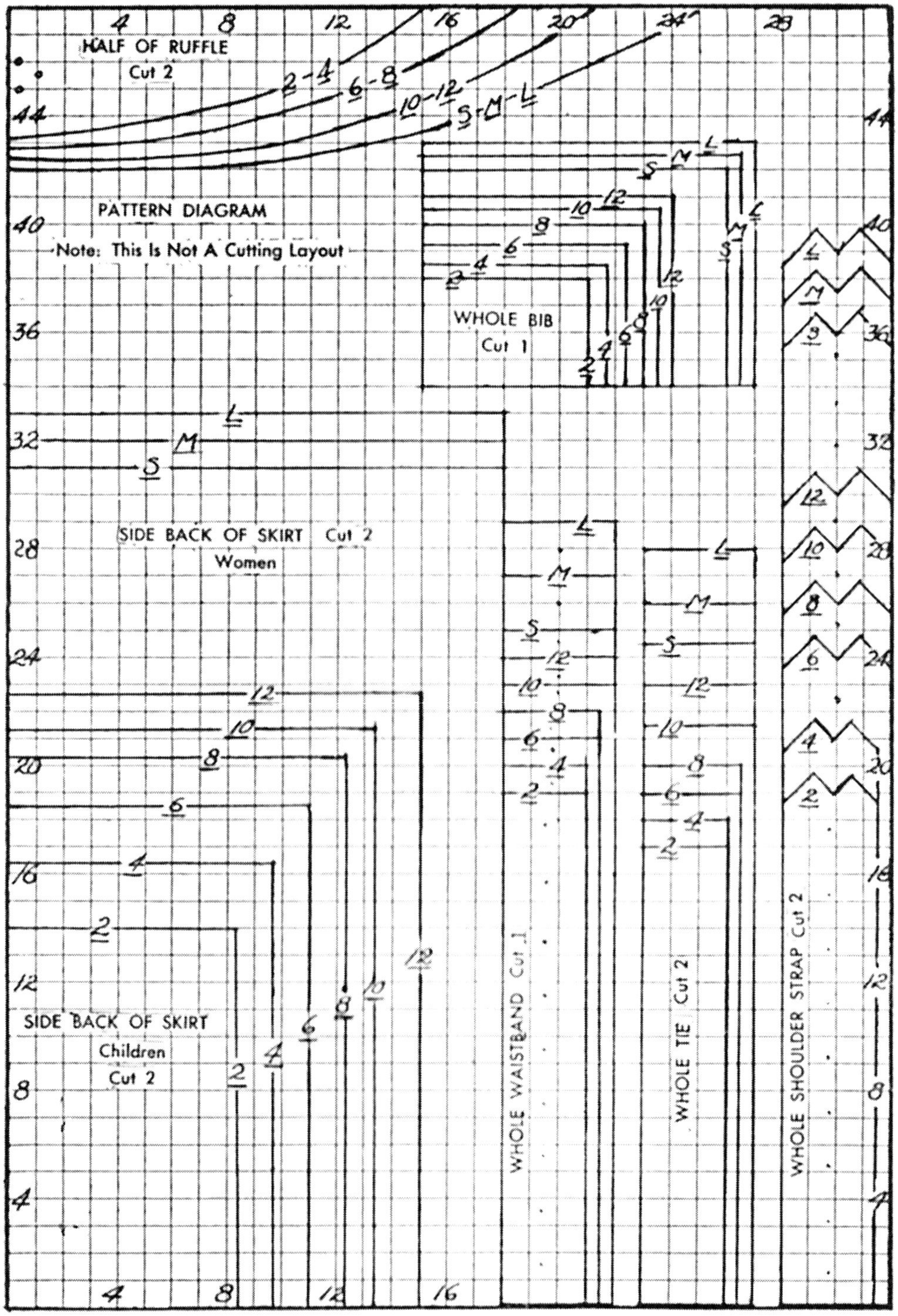
HALF OF RUFFLE
Cut 2
2-4
6-8
10-12
S-M-L
PATTERN DIAGRAM
Note: This Is Not A Cutting Layout
WHOLE BIB
Cut 1
SIDE BACK OF SKIRT Cut 2
Women
SIDE BACK OF SKIRT
Children
Cut 2
WHOLE WAISTBAND Cut 1
WHOLE TIE Cut 2
WHOLE SHOULDER STRAP Cut 2

**MATERIALS**

36-inch fabric; 2 buttons.

*For Children*

| | | | |
|---|---|---|---|
| Size 2: | 1½ yards | Size 8 : | 2⅛ yards |
| Size 4: | 1¾ yards | Size 10: | 2¼ yards |
| Size 6: | 2 yards | Size 12: | 2½ yards |

*For Women*

| *Apron with Ruffles* | | *Apron without Ruffles* | |
|---|---|---|---|
| Small: | 3⅛ yards | Small: | 2⅞ yards |
| Medium: | 3¼ yards | Medium: | 3 yards |
| Large: | 3⅜ yards | Large: | 3 yards |

**CUTTING**

Make pattern for individual size following pattern diagram. Underlined figures and letters indicate sizes. Lay pieces marked "cut 2" on double fabric. *In addition to pieces shown,* for all sizes, cut full width of fabric for skirt front, same length as side back of skirt. See cutting layout for suggested placement.

**SEWING**

1. Make 1½-inch hem in top of bib.
2. Hem sides of ties and *curved edges* of ruffles with machine hemmer (see page 114), or by hand. Make a 1-inch hem in one end of ties. If lace or other trim is to be used, apply to curved edges of ruffle.

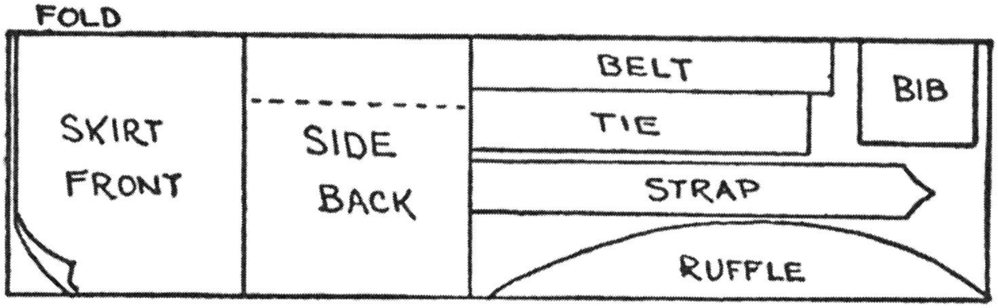

3. Fold shoulder straps lengthwise, sew pointed ends and turn inside out, making a center crease down entire length of strap.
4. Attach bib to open ends of straps as shown on page 113.
5. Gather shoulder ruffle and stitch to under edge of strap with wrong side of ruffle facing right side of strap, beginning at point approximately 2 inches above lower end of bib and stopping at point where straps normally cross in back, adjusting gathers to fit. Fold outside edge of strap over edges of ruffle, turning in all raw edges, and topstitch entire length of strap closed.
6. Make a small pinch pleat in each side of bib. Center bib on waistband and attach in manner shown on page 113.
7. Join side pieces of skirt to skirt front, using French seam or false French seam made with machine hemmer, as shown on page 112.
8. Make small hems in sides of skirt.
9. Gather skirt, drawing up to length ½ inch less than waistband.
10. Join skirt to back edge of waistband with wrong side of apron facing right side of band, and adjust gathers evenly.
11. Close band, folding in all raw edges ¼ inch, pleating and inserting ties in end of band at the same time. Topstitch in place.
12. Hand hem skirt to desired length (4-inch hem is allowed on all sizes).
13. Make vertical buttonholes in waistband at middle of each side of back and determine position of buttons on end of strap.

# Mother's Cobbler Dress

*(Small, Medium, and Large Sizes)*

Wraps around back, ties in front, and teams with Daughter's Cobbler Dress (page 40). *For pocket design see page 118.*

**MATERIALS**

Small (10-12): 4⅞ yards of 36-inch fabric. Medium (14-16): 5¼ yards of 36-inch fabric. Large (18-20): 5½ yards of 36-inch fabric.

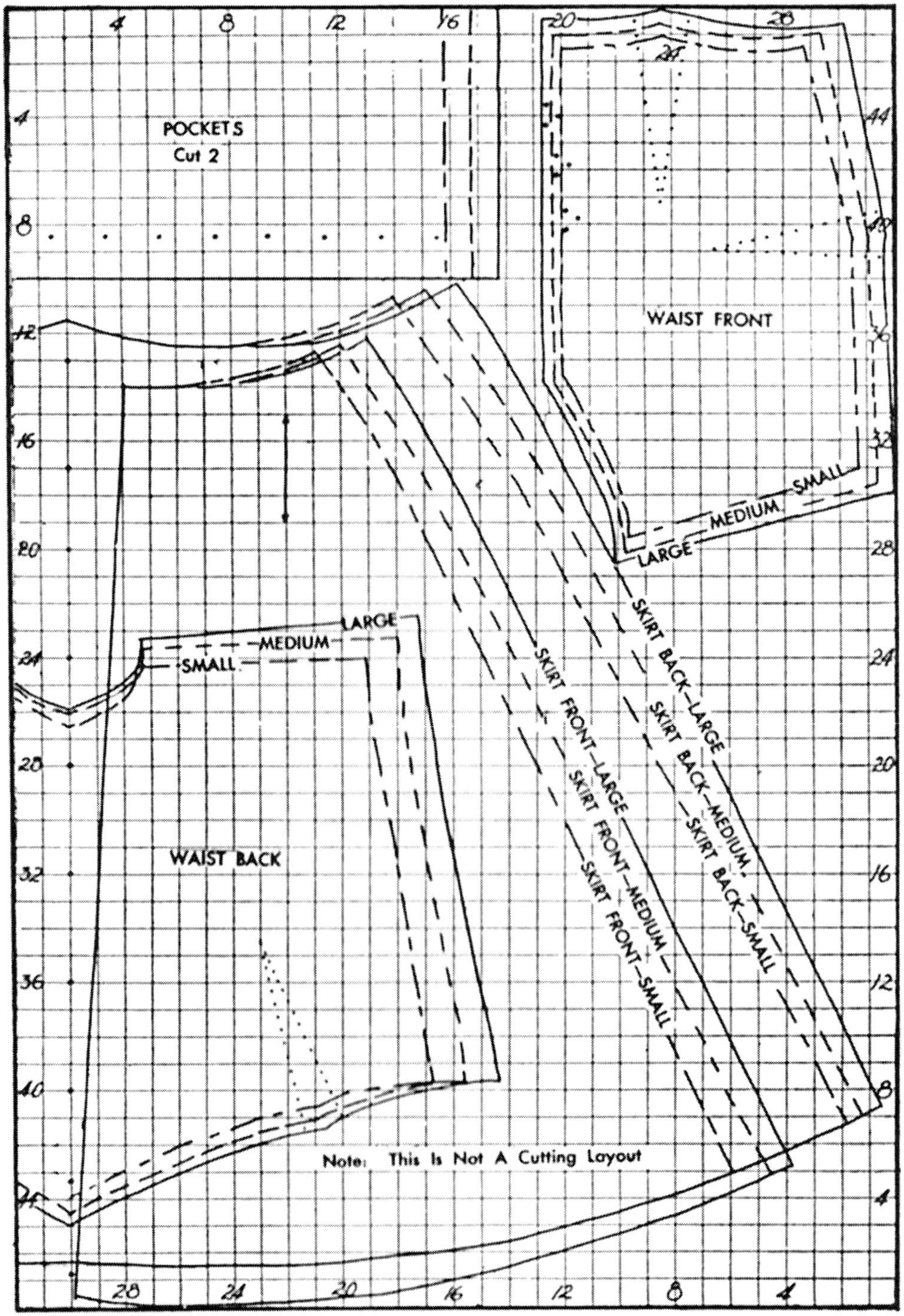

POCKETS
Cut 2
WAIST FRONT
LARGE
MEDIUM
SMALL
WAIST BACK
SKIRT FRONT—LARGE
SKIRT FRONT—MEDIUM
SKIRT FRONT—SMALL
SKIRT BACK—LARGE
SKIRT BACK—MEDIUM
SKIRT BACK—SMALL
Note: This Is Not A Cutting Layout

**CUTTING**

**Note.** This is not a cutting layout.

Make pattern for individual size using pattern diagram. *In addition to pieces shown,* cut 2 ties 4 inches wide and approximately 36 inches long. Cut waist front on fold, and waist backs and skirt backs on selvage edge. Arrow shows straight of goods for skirt front pieces.

**SEWING**

1. Make 1-inch hems in tops of pocket pieces. Fold in lower edge ¼ inch.
2. Measure down 14½ inches from curved tops of skirt fronts and apply lower edges of pocket pieces. Topstitch.
3. Baste edges of pocket pieces to center edges of skirt fronts. Stitch each pocket in center, dividing in two.
4. Stitch center front seam.
5. Make darts in front and back waist.
6. Join shoulder seams.
7. Fold in and tack hems on back edges of waist and skirt, following dots.
8. Turn in top of skirt front ½ inch and topstitch to waist top. Do same with back skirts and waist tops.
9. Join side seams from underarm darts to lower edge of skirt, leaving a 2-inch opening at waistline in right side seam.
10. Hem or face armhole edges and face neck edge.
11. Fold ties in half lengthwise, stitch, and turn.
12. Attach ties to each side of back waistline.
13. Hem skirt to desired length.
14. Place button and buttonhole at back neck edge.

## Daughter's Cobbler Dress

(*Size 6—Adjustable to Sizes 4 and 8*)

This can be worn as an apron or as a coverall dress. *For appliqué see page 119.*

**MATERIALS**

Size 4: 1⅝ yards of 36-inch fabric. Size 6: 1⅞ yards. Size 8: 2 yards. All sizes: 1¾ yards bias tape; 7 buttons.

**CUTTING**

**Note.** This is not a cutting layout.

Make pattern from diagram, adjusting sizes as follows: for size 4, cut ¼ inch off shoulder and side and 4 inches off skirt; for size 8, add ¼ inch on shoulder, ⅜ inch on side, ⅛ inch at center front and back, and 4 inches at hem. *In addition to pieces shown on diagram,* cut 2 ties, 4 inches by 28 inches and pocket piece, 7 inches wide and 25 inches long for size 4, 26 inches for size 6, and 28 inches for size 8.

**SEWING**

1. Make ¾-inch hem in one long edge of pocket piece. Turn in

other long edge ¼-inch and topstitch to apron front along curved line of dots, raising line 1 inch for size 4 and lowering it 1½ inches for size 8. Baste ends of piece to side edges of apron to be caught later in side seams.

2. Stitch a vertical line in center of pocket piece, dividing it into two parts. Divide each part in half again, adjusting top fullness evenly.
3. Turn in back edges of apron along dots and tack in place.
4. Join shoulder seams and side seams.
5. Bind neck and sleeve edges with bias tape.
6. Make small hem in each long side of ties and ½-inch hem in one short end. Make darts as shown by dots at waistline, at the same time pleating and inserting ends of ties. Raise or lower darts according to size.
7. Hem to desired length (3 inches allowed). Close back with buttons and buttonholes, adjusting spacing according to size.

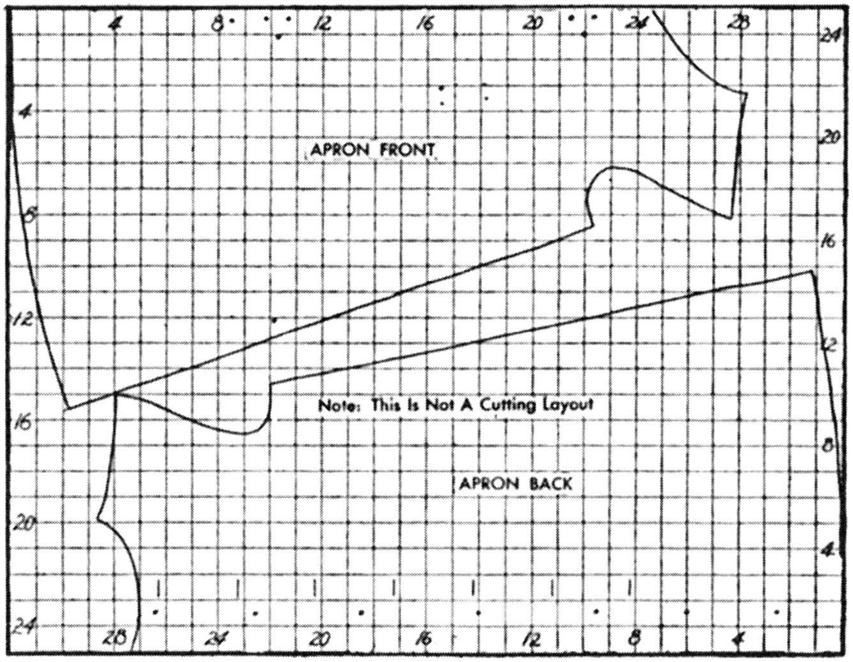

# Cover-Up Nursery Apron

*(Size 1-2)*

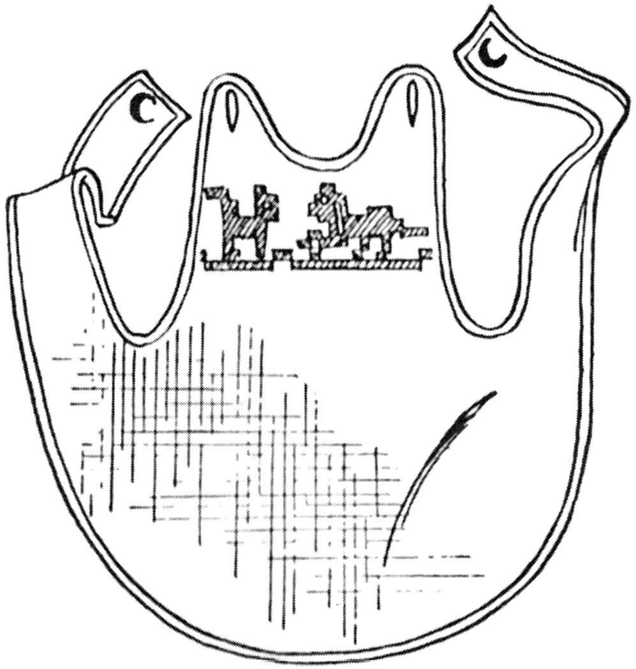

Straps cross in back and button to the front tabs. If you use checked gingham, it will serve as a guide for tiny cross-stitch motifs.

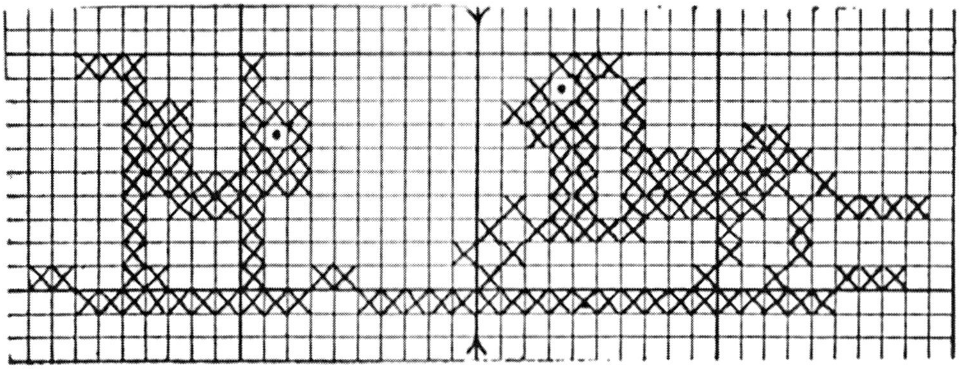

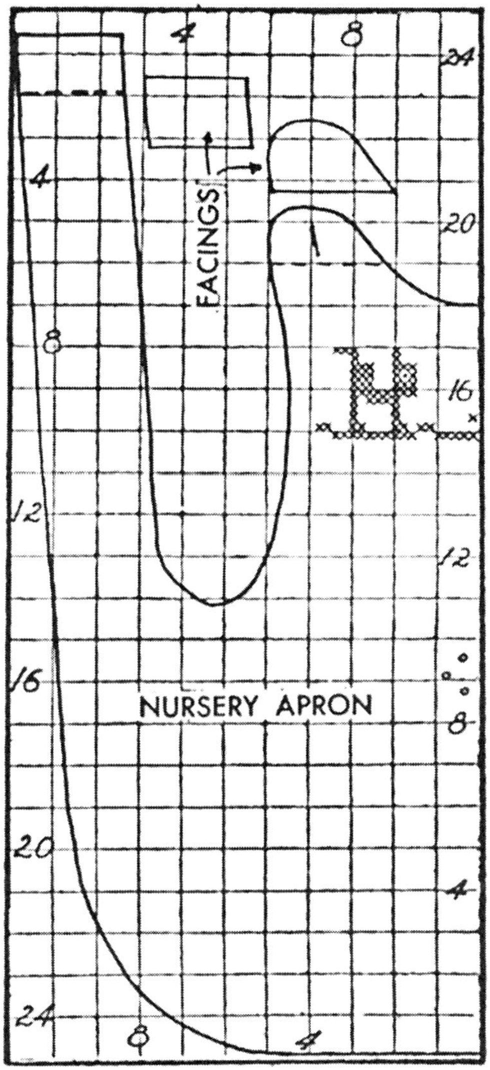


**MATERIALS**

1 piece of checked gingham, 22 by 24 inches (about 5 checks to 1 inch); 3½ yards of double-fold bias tape; two buttons; embroidery floss.

**CUTTING**

Use cutting layout.

**SEWING**

1. Baste facing to front tab and strap ends, topstitching lower edges in place.
2. Bind entire outer edge with bias tape.
3. Make buttonhole vertically in center of each front tab and sew buttons to strap ends.
4. Using squares of gingham as guide, center cross-stitch motif in position shown, and work with contrasting floss.

# Infant's Feeding Apron

(*Size 1-2*)

This apron can be made short, with a "crumb pocket," or long enough to cover a high-chair tray or table edge.

**MATERIALS**

*Short apron:* ¾ yard of 36-inch plastic material; 2½ double-fold yards of bias tape. *Long version:* 1⅛ yards of 36-inch material; 3½ yards tape. Either version ⅜ yard of elastic.

**CUTTING**

Use cutting layout. For short apron cut along dotted line.

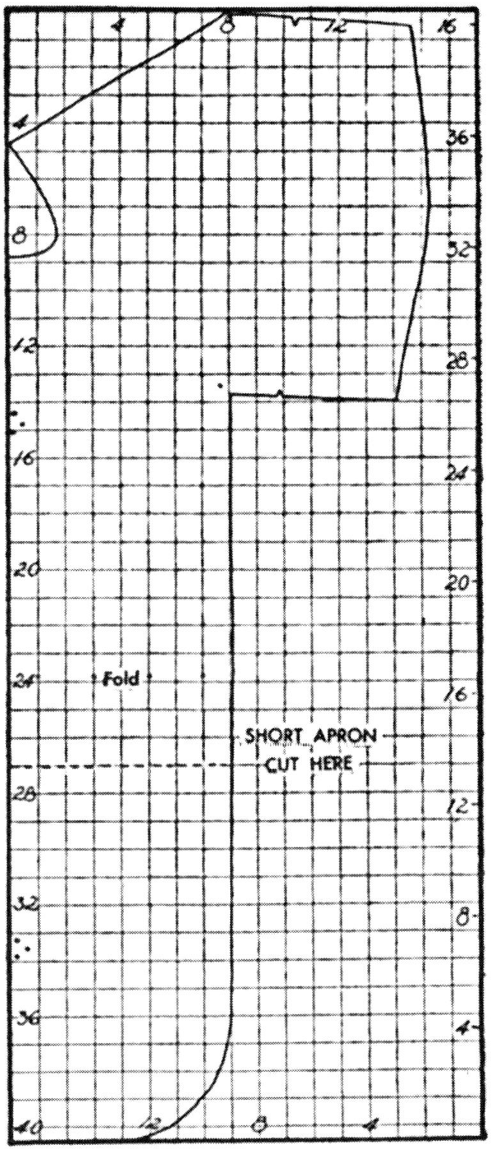


**SEWING**

**Note.** To sew plastic see page 115.

1. For short apron, bind across bottom and fold toward front along dotted line to form pocket.
2. Seam sleeve and slash underarm to dot, matching notches.
3. Beginning at center back, bind completely around outer edge, except neckline.
4. Make an 8-inch tie by doubling bias, continue with same piece of bias to bind neck edge and end other side with another 8-inch tie.
5. Finish bottom of sleeves with ⅜ inch hem leaving small opening. Insert elastic and draw up to desired measure.

# One-Yard Aprons

BIAS APRON

APRON WITH BACK YOKE

# One-Yard Bias Apron

*(Medium Size)*

**MATERIALS**

1 yard of 36-inch fabric; 6 yards of bias binding (optional).

**CUTTING**

**Note.** Each square on this diagram equals 2 inches.

Use cutting layout with center front on bias fold.

**SEWING**

1. Hem or bind edges of ties, and the complete outside edge of apron and top edge of pocket.
2. Baste darts, inserting belts as indicated. (Apron may be gathered to fit and belt sewn down along dotted line, or belt simply tied in back.)
3. Join bias strips for neck strap and adjust to desired length. Attach to top of apron.
4. Turn in raw edges of pocket ¼ inch and topstitch in position shown.

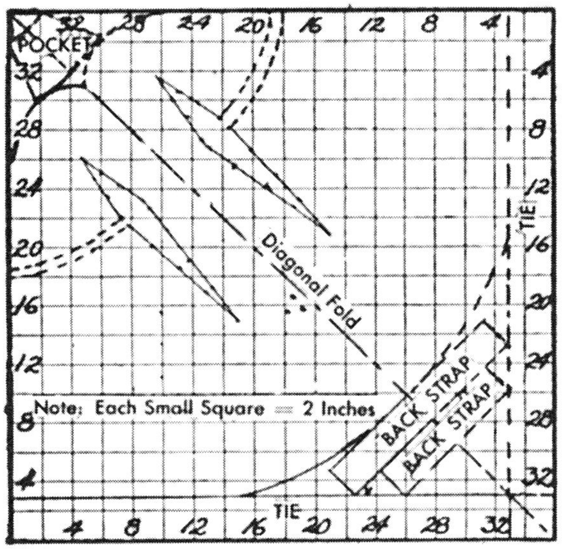

# One-Yard Apron with Back Yoke

(*Medium Size*)

**MATERIALS**

1 yard of 36-inch fabric; 7½ yards of bias binding.

**CUTTING**

Use cutting layout with center front on fold.

**SEWING**

1. Attach ties, matching notches.
2. Join center back of yoke and shoulder seams, matching notches.
3. Bind entire *outer* edge including belts.
4. Bind neck edge and top edge of pocket.
5. Turn in raw edge of pocket ¼ inch and topstitch to apron, following dots.

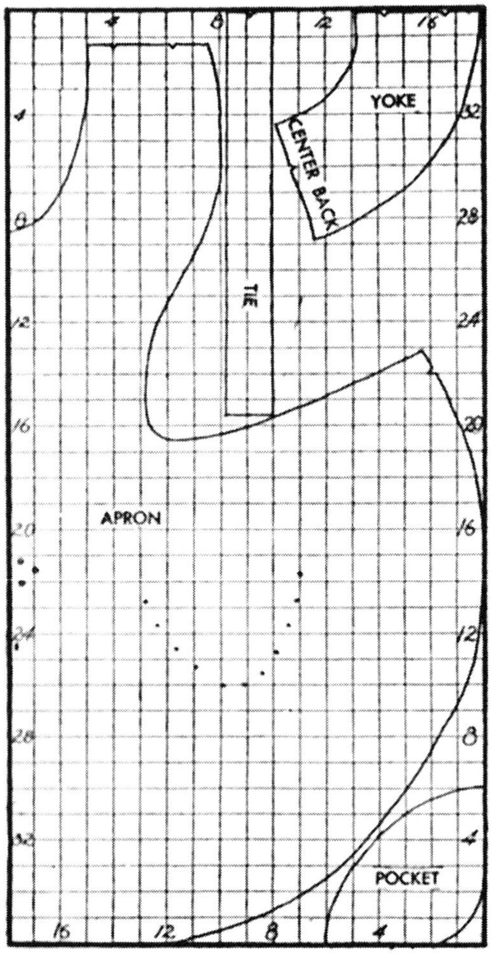

# One-Yard Gored Apron

*(Medium Size)*

Shoulder straps and ties join at center back of waist to hold apron firmly in place.

**MATERIALS**

1 yard of 36-inch fabric; 5 yards of bias tape.

**CUTTING**

Use cutting layout with center front on fold.

**SEWING**

1. Bind top edges of pockets. Place on side pieces of apron, matching notches, turn in curved edge ¼ inch and topstitch.

2. Seam side pieces to front matching notches.
3. Bind all outer edges including bottom, with bias tape.
4. Fold shoulder straps lengthwise, stitch, and turn.
5. With back piece folded, sew sides, leaving end open. Turn. Attach one end of strap to each side of top of apron at "A" on diagram; insert other end in top of back piece. Turn in and stitch back piece closed.
6. Hem each tie on two sides and one end and attach raw ends to apron at "B" on diagram, pleating in ties before sewing.
7. Make two 1½-inch buttonholes in back piece (short heavy lines on diagram). Pass ties through buttonholes and tie.

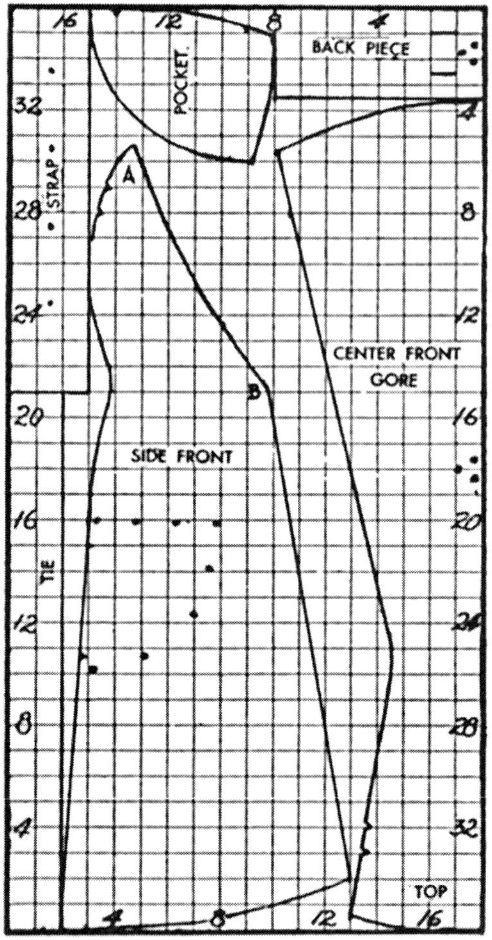

## Triangular Tea Apron

*(One Size)*

Can be made with or without halter bib, tying at the neck.

**MATERIALS**

29 inches of 32-inch taffeta or other suitable fabric; 4 yards of ½-inch trimming.

**CUTTING**

Using cutting layout, cut ties first and then fold fabric on the bias and cut apron and pocket. Cut other parts out of remaining straight piece.

**SEWING**

1. Hem tops of bib and pocket and edges of apron front, folding along dots.
2. Apply trimming over the hemming lines.
3. Make small hem on long edges of ties and 1-inch hem on one end.
4. Turn in edges of pockets and topstitch to apron.

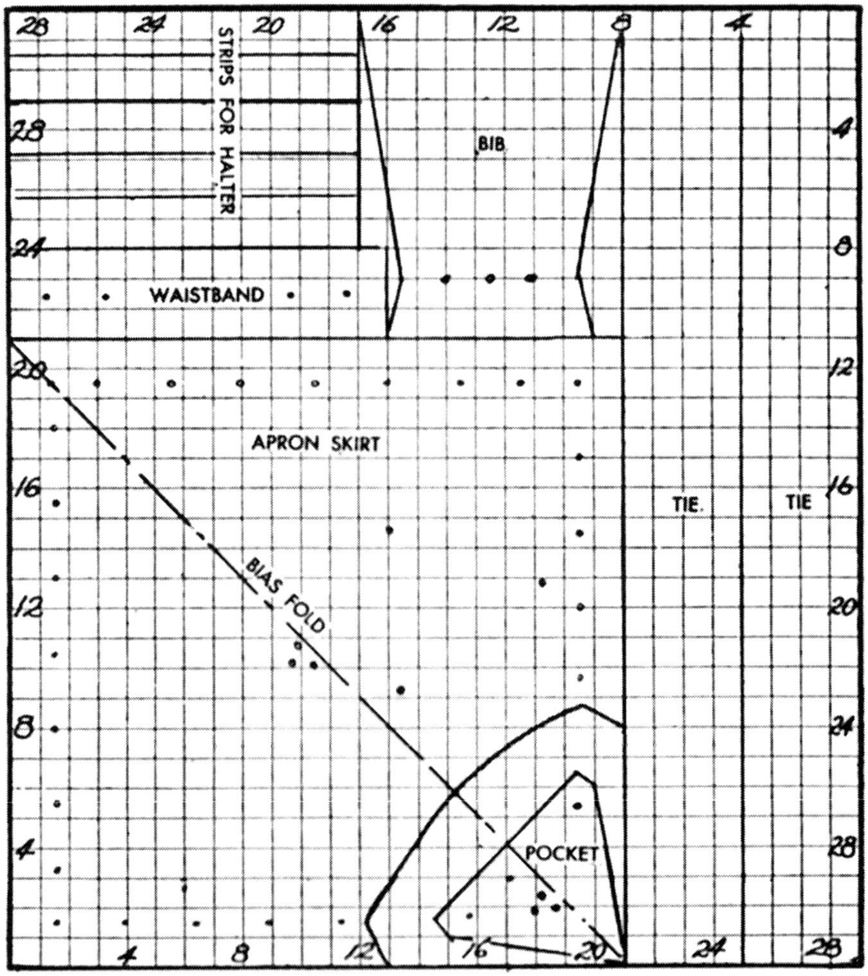


5. Join strips for halter ties end to end. Divide in half.
6. With right sides together, join halters to sides of bib. Fold halters lengthwise, turn in raw edges, and whip down to back of bib. Continue, whipping closed their entire length. Apply trimming.
7. Center and attach bib to waistband as shown on page 113.
8. With right sides together, center and attach apron front to waistband. Whip down waistband on underside, pleating and inserting raw ends of ties in ends of waistband.

## Cobbler Apron

(*Size 18—Adjustable to Sizes 16 and 14*)

This sleeveless short coverall apron has a whole row of pockets. It buttons at the back of the neck. *For rick-rack embroidery see page 125.*

**MATERIALS**

2 yards of 36-inch fabric; 5 yards of bias binding.

**CUTTING**

**Note.** This is not a cutting layout.

Make back pattern by solid line, cut with center back of pattern on selvage. Make front and ties by dotted line. Cut front and pocket pattern on center fold, ties on edge. Make darts in front only. To adjust pattern for size 16, trim ½ inch from shoulder, armhole, side, and back neck edge. Alter front neck edge only at bottom. For size 14, trim 1 inch instead of ½ inch at the same points.

**SEWING**

1. Fold in center back hems at line of dots and tack in place.
2. Face top edge of pocket piece and join to lower edge of front with right side of pocket facing wrong side of front. Turn. Baste in position at sides.
3. Join shoulder seams and underarm seams.
4. Fold ties lengthwise, stitch, and turn.
5. Make darts, inserting ties into darts at the waistline at the same time.
6. Face neck and armholes and lower back edges.
7. Make lines of stitching as shown, dividing pockets into five parts.

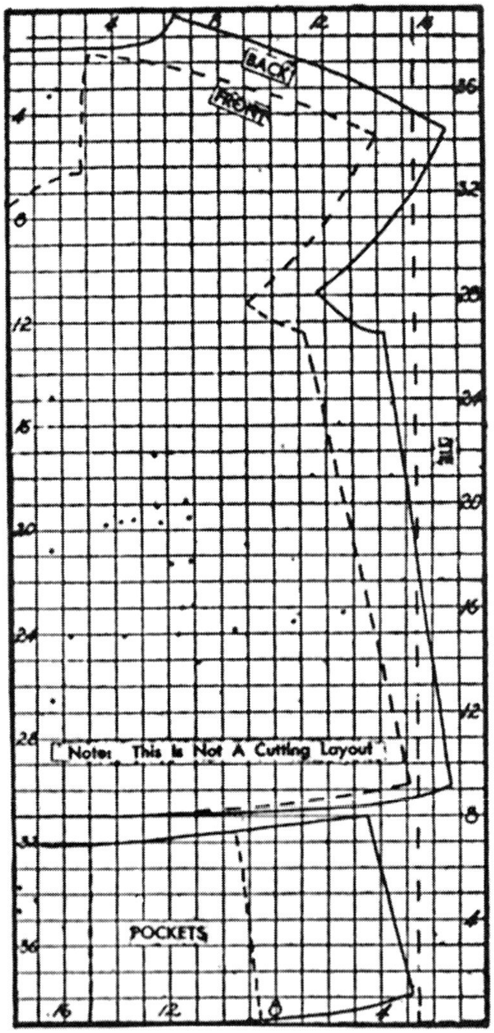

## Apron for the Mature Figure

(*Sizes 38-42 and 44-48*)

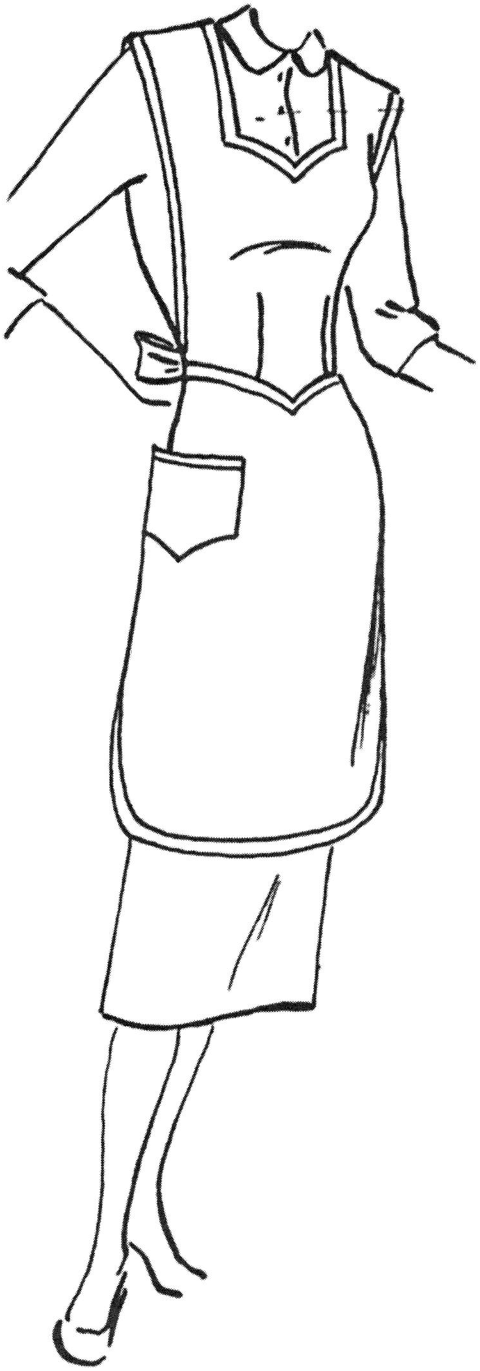

An apron designed to flatter the more mature figure.

**MATERIALS**

Sizes 38-42: 1⅝ yards of 36-inch fabric. Sizes 44-48: 1¾ yards. 7 yards of bias tape.

**CUTTING**

**Note.** This is not a cutting layout.

Make pattern using solid line for smaller size, dotted line for larger one. Lay pieces on center fold as indicated, piecing skirt where necessary. *In addition to pieces shown,* cut ties 32 inches long and about 4 inches wide.

**SEWING**

1. Make darts in apron top. Seam back yoke and apron top at the shoulders.
2. Bind outside edge of top, neck edge, top of pocket, and around entire skirt, including top of skirt.
3. Center skirt on top lapping ½ inch over bottom edge of top, stitching just inside binding line.
4. Make small hem on long edges of ties and a 1-inch hem in one end of each. Pleat raw ends and insert tie into each corner formed by top and skirt, stitching to top and skirt both, just inside binding line.

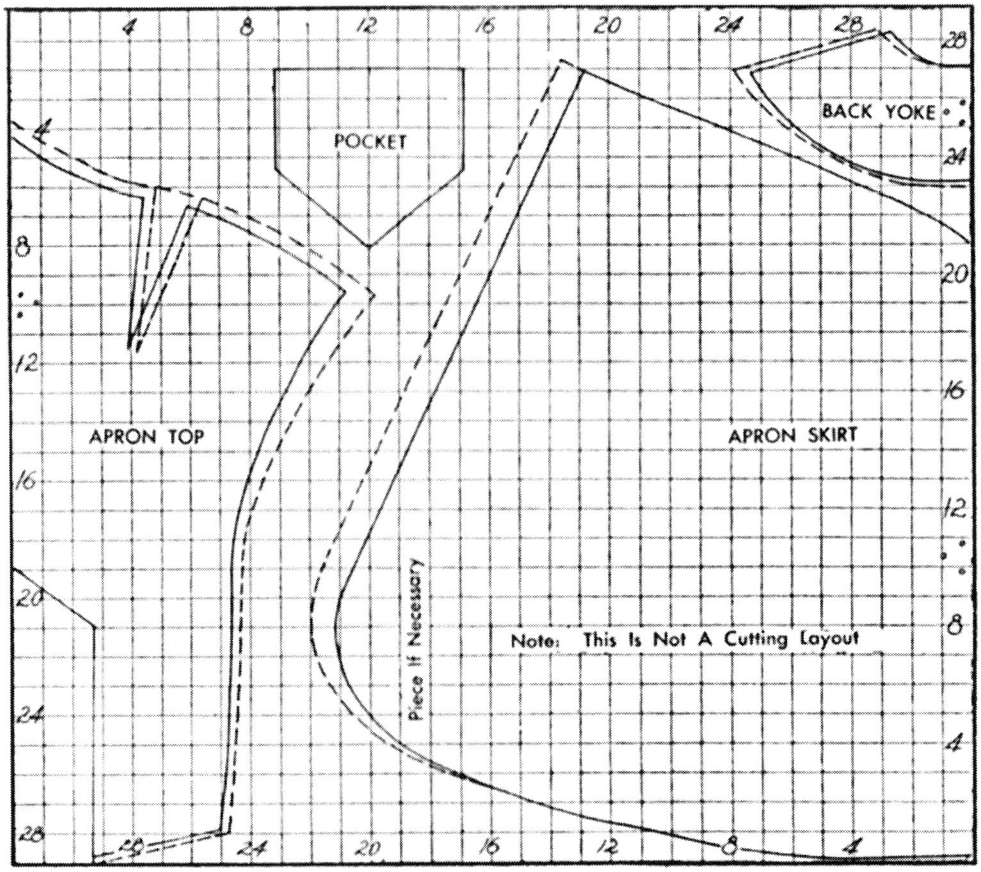

# Baby-Bathing Apron

A towel, a washcloth, and a minimum of sewing make this useful apron.

**MATERIALS**

Turkish bath towel 22 by 36 inches; matching wash cloth; 4½ yards of 1½-inch folded sateen blanket binding.

**CUTTING**

*Ties and waistband:* Cut blanket binding 2½ yards long with slanting ends. *Neck strap:* Cut blanket binding 21 inches long.

**SEWING**

1. Gather one long side of towel to measure 12 inches.
2. Center gathered edge of skirt on back open edge of waistband and stitch.
3. Center washcloth (bib) and attach as shown on page 113.
4. Topstitch, closing waistband and ties.
5. Bind top edge of bib and lower edge of skirt, stitching around all edges of binding.
6. Stitch sides of neck strap and sew ends to top of bib.

# Bibbed Apron with Back Cross Straps

*(Medium Size)*

This fitted apron opens out flat for easy ironing. *For appliqué see page 119.*

**MATERIALS**

1⅛ yards of 36-inch fabric; 3 yards of rickrack braid or bias facing.

**CUTTING**

Use cutting layout with skirt and yoke pieces on center fold. Open out material to cut shoulder straps. To adjust size, add or subtract to center front and side edges of bib and skirt and ends of straps.

**SEWING**

1. Finish top edge of bib, sides, and bottom of skirt with rick-rack or bias facing as desired.

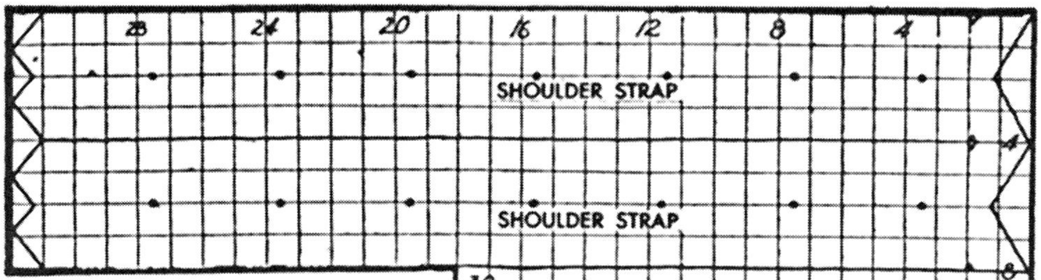


2. Sew and turn pointed ends of straps.
3. Fold straps, and insert back side edges of bib at matching notches. Turn in ¼ inch and baste strap closed. Topstitch straps on folded edge, around point, and down basted side.
4. Make darts in apron skirt. Hem pocket and topstitch to matching dots.
5. Gather bottom of bib between notches. Join skirt and bib, lapping skirt over yoke. Topstitch.
6. Make buttonholes in end of straps and sew buttons to top of bib.

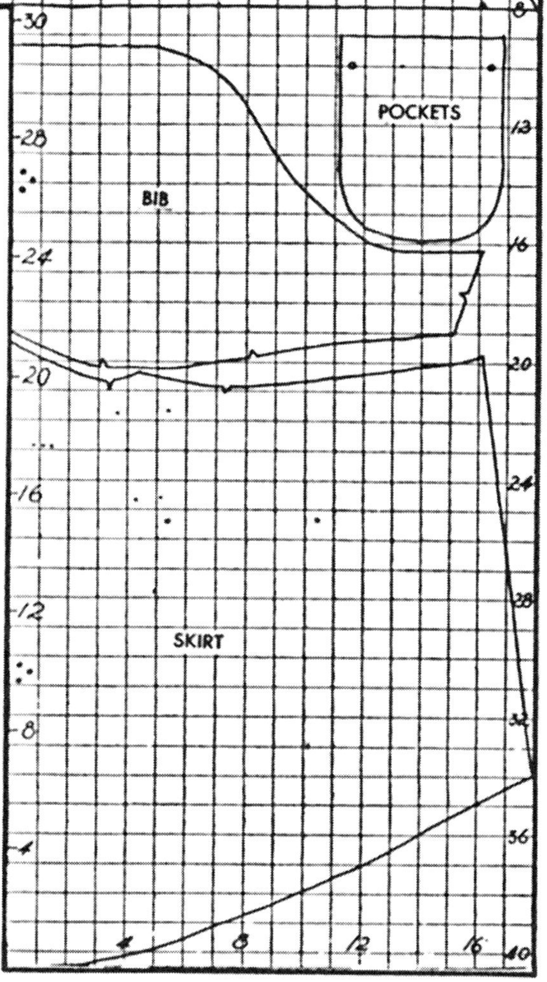

# Half Aprons from Three-Quarters Yard of Fabric

One version is gored, the other gathered. Either may be decorated in many different ways. *For appliqué designs see page 116. For cross-stitch see page 123.*

**MATERIALS**

¾ yard of 36-inch fabric for either view, or make gored apron from remnants, using contrasting materials for the gores. Bias binding (optional).

**CUTTING**

See cutting layout. Cut on lines indicated for gored apron. For gathered apron, disregard lines for gores, leaving skirt in a single piece. Ties are the same for both aprons. Note different waistband lengths; A is for gored apron and B is for gathered apron.

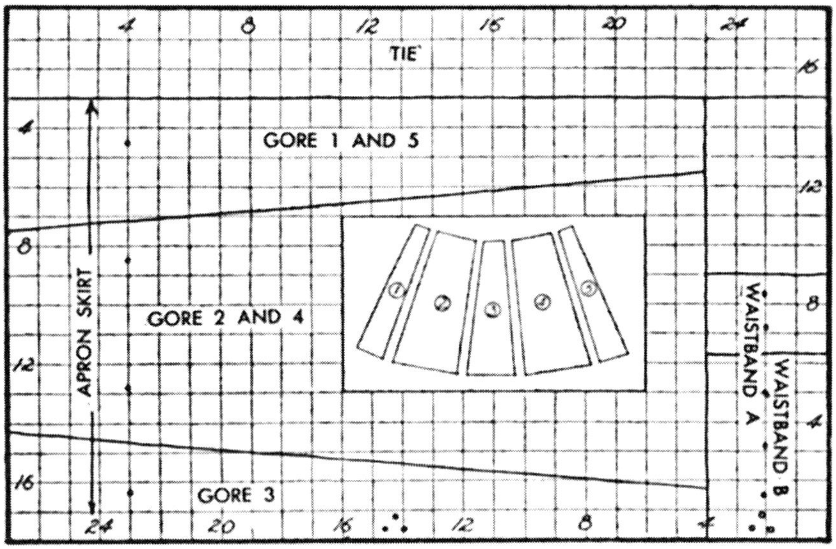


## SEWING

### Gored Apron

1. Arrange gores as shown in small insert diagram and join.
2. Hem or bind around entire outside edge of apron.
3. Make ¼-inch hem in sides of ties and 1-inch hem at one end of each tie.
4. Attach apron to edge of waistband (A on diagram), and turn band. Pleat and insert ties at ends and stitch band in place.

### Gathered Apron

1. Make ¼-inch hem at sides of apron and 4-inch hem at bottom as shown by dots on diagram.
2. Hem ties as in step 3 for gored apron.
3. Gather in top of apron to 12 inches and attach to waistband (B on diagram).
4. Attach apron to edge of belt, turn belt and finish in same manner as gored apron.

# Gathered Half Apron

This pattern, so simple that it needs no diagram, can be varied with a false hem of a contrasting fabric. *For iron-on appliqué, see page 122.*

**MATERIALS**

1 yard and 24 inches of 36-inch fabric *OR* 1 yard and 12 inches of one color and 24 inches of another color for false hem.

**CUTTING**

Cut two lengths of fabric 30 inches long. From side of one piece (center front), cut waistband 4 inches wide and 24 inches long. Cut two ties 4 inches wide from sides of other piece. Split remaining portion of this piece in half for sides of apron. If apron with contrasting hem is desired, cut pieces same as above but 24 inches long for top of apron, and, of contrasting fabric for false hem, cut portions 12 inches long and as wide as top panels.

**SEWING**

1. Join sides and front of apron, using French seam or hemmer French seam (see page 112). If false hem is being used, join panels for top and hem in same way and join in crosswise seam with right sides together.
2. Make narrow hems on sides of apron and a 6-inch hem in lower edge. For false hem, fold hem in half, whipping over the joining seam.
3. Gather top of apron to measure ½ inch less than waistband. Center gathered edge on waistband with wrong sides of apron to right side of waistband, adjust gathering evenly and stitch. (If waistband is to be finished by hand, place apron on waistband with right sides facing, so that edge may be hand whipped on wrong side instead of stitched on right side in step 5.)
4. Make small hem on each side of ties and a one inch hem on one end of each tie.
5. Fold band over gathers, turning in all raw edges ¼ inch, pleat ties to fit finished waistband width, insert ties in ends of waistband, and topstitch waistband closed.

## Smocked Half Apron

**MATERIALS**

Same as gathered half apron (page 62); plus six-strand embroidery floss.

**CUTTING**

Cut same as gathered half apron, omitting waistband.

**SEWING**

1. Join pieces and hem apron in the same way as for gathered half apron, making a small hem in top edge also.
2. For *smocking* prepare fabric by drawing dots according to spacing shown on page 126, beginning at a point 1 inch below finished top edge and continuing for a depth of 4 inches, *or* use a smocking hot-iron transfer. Embroider as shown in stitch diagram on page 126, using 2 strands of floss.
3. Finish ties in the same way as for gathered half apron, and attach to sides of apron, centering on smocking.

# Aprons with Shaped Yokes

1A

2A

There are many yoke shapes with which to vary the design of half aprons. The upper edge of the yoke presents no problem, but the lower edge and top of apron to be attached to it, must be shaped to fit together. The following diagrams show you how to fit any yoke shape you may desire for either a gathered or flared apron. *For detached appliqué see page 121.*

**CUTTING**

1. Draw pattern showing desired yoke shape and length of apron without fullness (see diagrams 1 and 2).
2. Cut yoke pattern and lower apron pattern apart.
3. Cut lower section into strips. Number as shown.
4. Spread out strips to desired fullness as shown. (Note that in 1A, flared apron, top corners of pieces are touching.

5. Draw around strips, and then draw line averaging top shapings.
6. Determine seam allowances and draw final cutting line. Pattern to fit any yoke shape may be made in the same way.

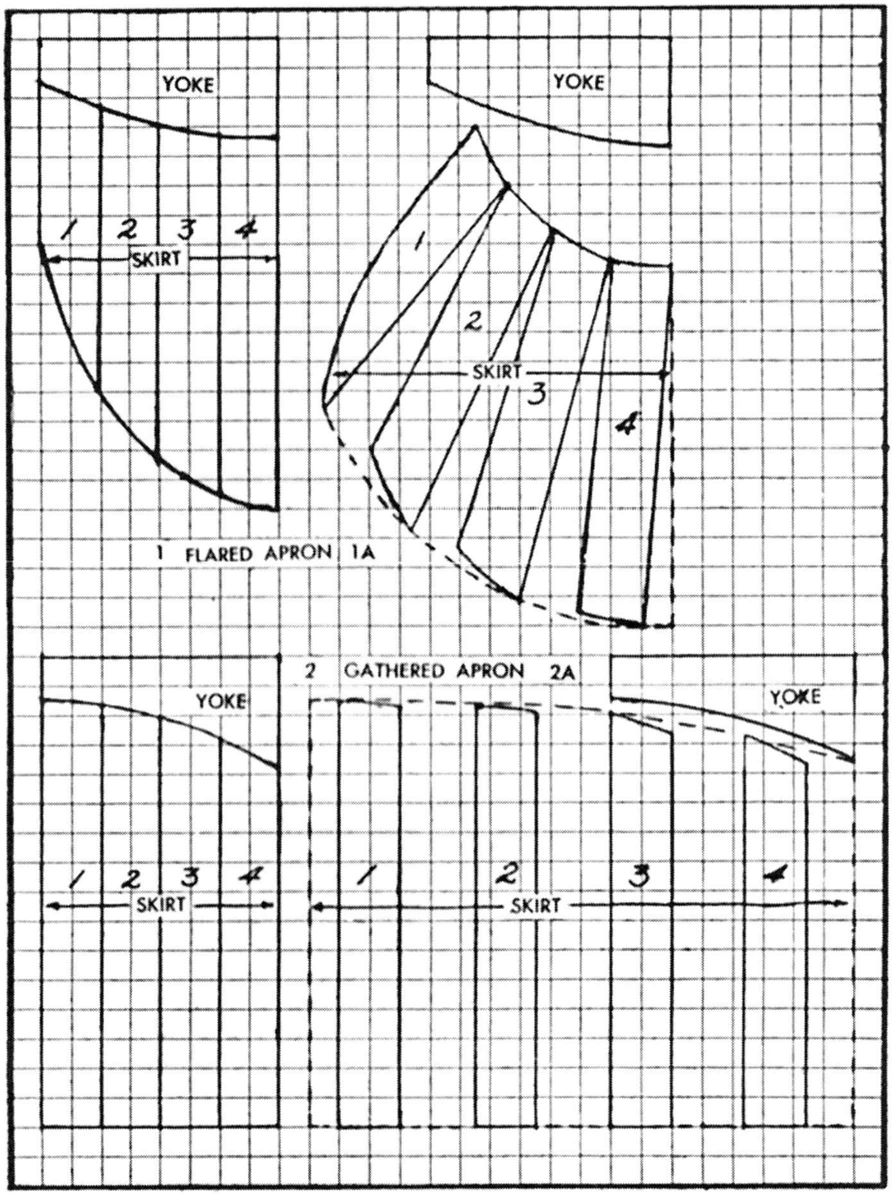

## Shirt-Tail Apron

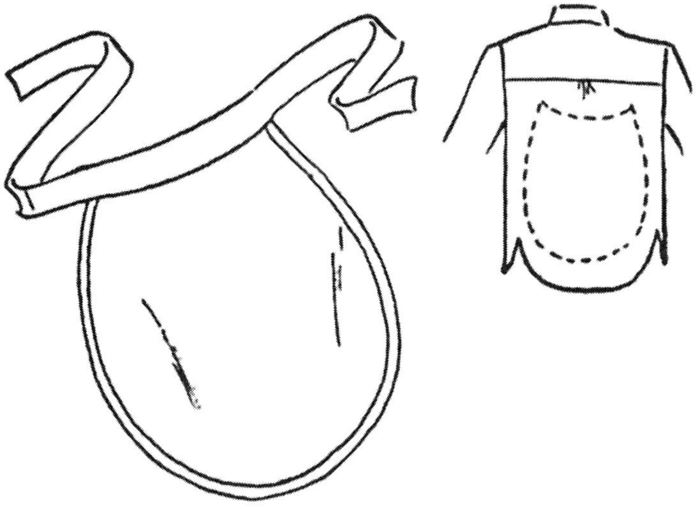

This apron is designed to be cut without piecing, from an average-sized man's shirt.

**MATERIALS**

One average-sized man's shirt *OR* 24 inches of 36-inch fabric; 2 yards bias facing, rickrack, or bias binding.

**CUTTING**

Cutting layout for fabric is shown. If a shirt is used, cut apron front from back of shirt and 3 pieces 24 inches long and 3½ inches wide from sleeves or right front.

**SEWING**

1. Finish edge of apron with bias facing, rickrack, or binding.
2. Join three 24-inch strips end to end, forming waistband and ties.
3. With wrong side of apron facing right side of waistband center and stitch apron on waistband.
4. Close waistband and ties, turning in all raw edges and top-stitching. Trim as desired.

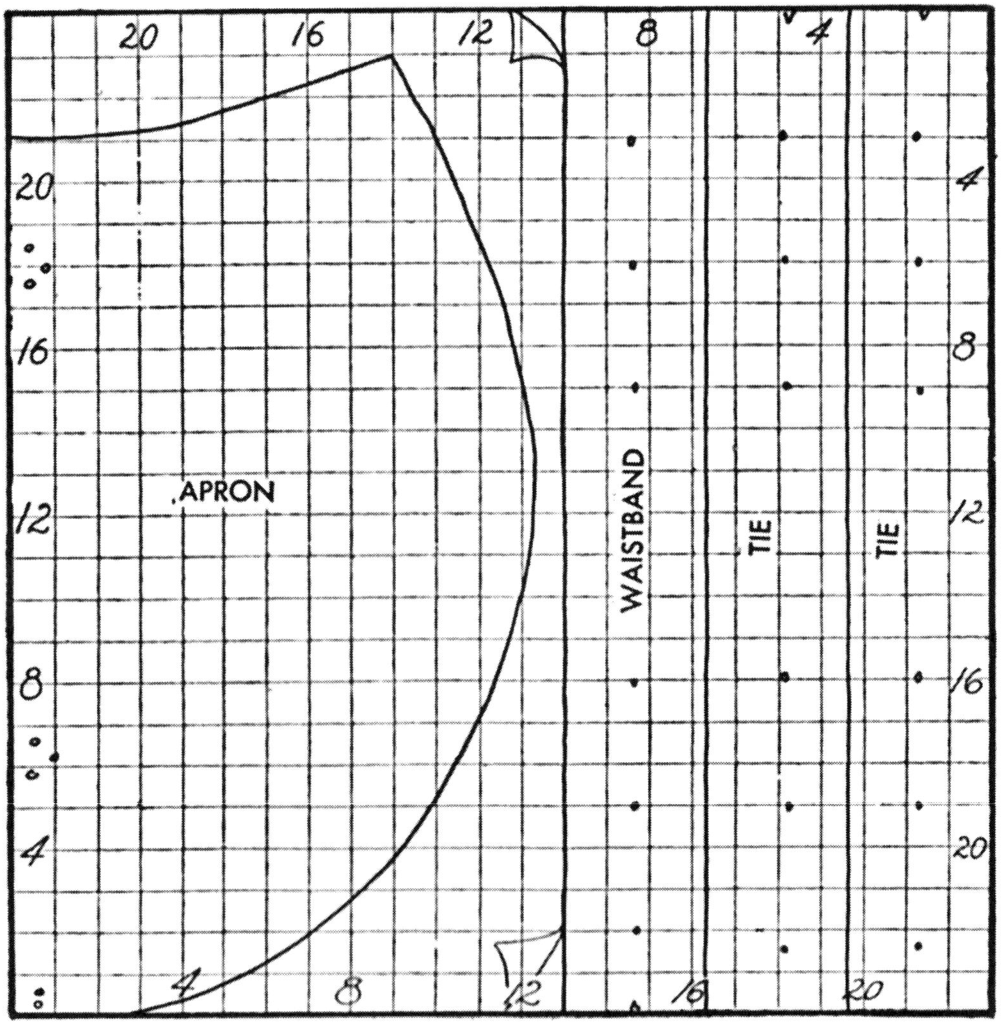


PATTERN FOR SHIRT-TAIL AND PICKER'S APRON

# Picker's Apron

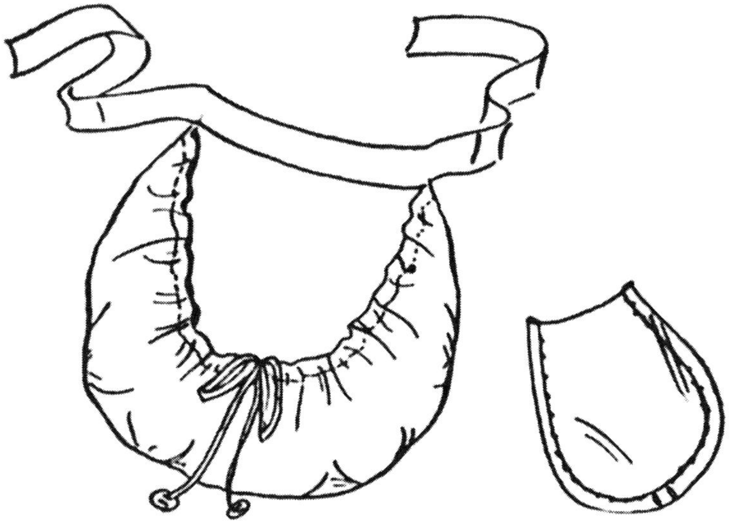

For the gal with a garden. Pull up and tie the strings and you'll have a nice temporary basket for vegetables or flowers.

**MATERIALS**

The same as for the shirt-tail apron (page 67); plus 1¾ yards of ½ inch twill tape and two ¾-inch buttons.

**CUTTING**

Use cutting layout for shirt-tail apron.

**SEWING**

1. Face edge of apron, turning facing toward front, and stitch making two openings one inch apart at bottom of apron.
2. Cut tape in 2 pieces, and thread through facing, one on each side to openings at bottom. Secure one end of each tape at top of apron, so that it will be caught in when waistband is stitched. Sew buttons on ends of tape where it comes out of opening at bottom.
3. Join ties and waistband as for shirt-tail apron on page 67.

## Round Ruffled Half Apron

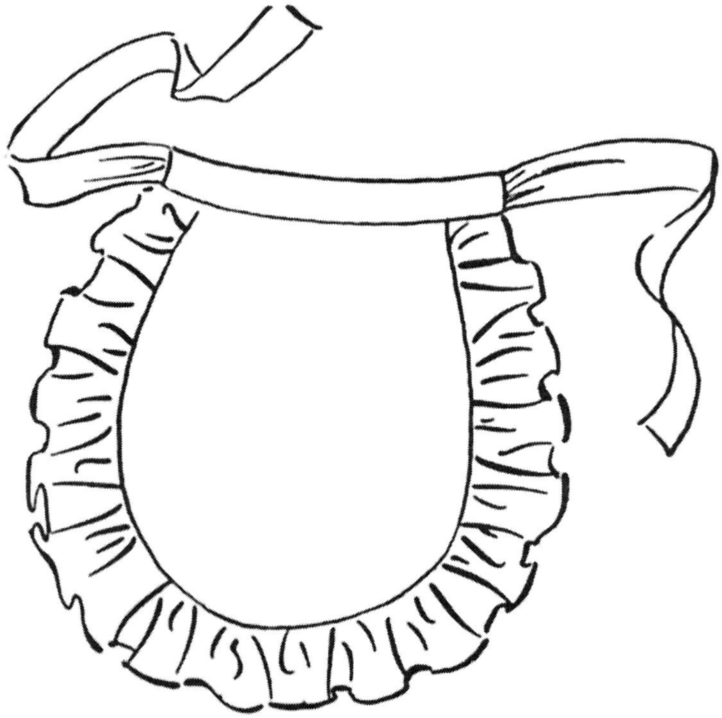

It was an apron not unlike this one, though undoubtedly somewhat more capacious, that Marie Antoinette wore when she played milkmaid at the Petit Trianon.

**MATERIALS**

1 yard and 15 inches of 36-inch fabric; five yards of lace (optional).

**CUTTING**

Use cutting layout. *In addition to the layout shown,* cut three more 5-inch crosswise strips for ruffling. If contrasting ruffle is desired, cut between 4 and 5 running yards of 5-inch strips. (Always cut ruffles crosswise of fabric as it gathers better than when cut lengthwise.)

**SEWING**

1. Join ruffle strips end to end in one continuous piece.
2. Hem ruffles with small hem, see page 112 for use of machine hemmer, and if lace or trimming is to be used, apply to ruffles.
3. Gather ruffles and baste to edge of apron, distributing fullness evenly. Stitch and overcast seam. Apply trimming to this seamline if desired.
4. Make a small hem in long edges of ties and a 1-inch hem on one end of each.
5. Center top of apron on back of waistband with wrong side of apron facing right side of band.
6. Close and topstitch band over apron and ruffles, adjusting length of the waistband if necessary, turning in all raw edges, and pleating and inserting ties in ends at the same time.

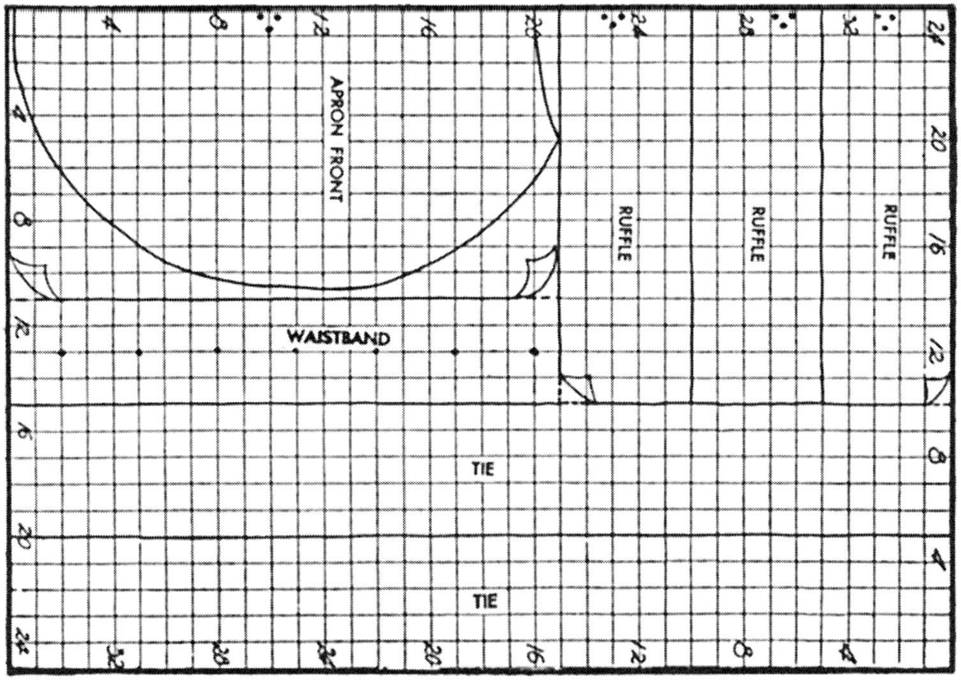

# Plastic Dusting and Pick-Up Apron

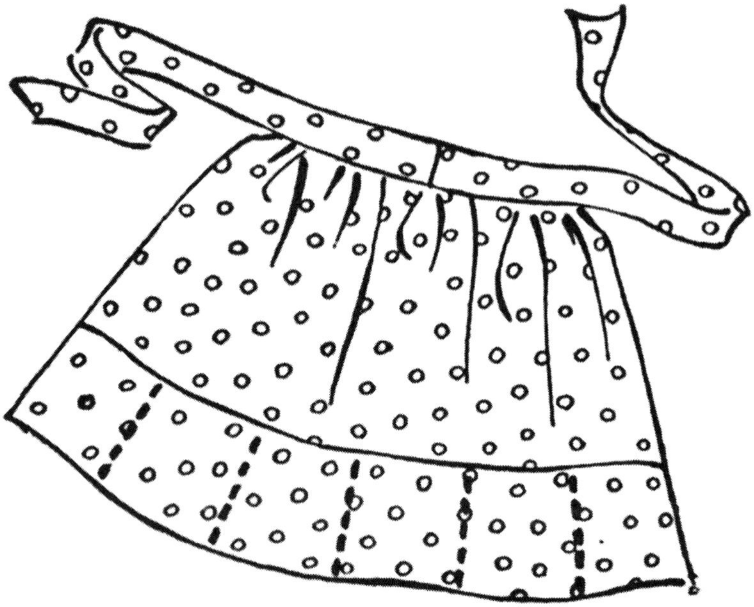

Here is an apron to put on when you do that quick morning whisking through the house, emptying ashtrays, giving the furniture a quick once-over, and picking up the innumerable little misplaced objects and bits of paper. It has a pocket to fit a sandwich sack to hold ashes and debris, one for a damp cloth, one for the dustcloth, another for the polish cloth, and two for good measure, into which go oddments to be put away later in their proper places.

**MATERIALS**

30 inches of 36-inch plastic material.

**CUTTING**

Follow cutting layout.

**SEWING**

See page 115 for hints on sewing plastic material.

1. Make a 1-inch hem on one long side of pocket piece.
2. Lay raw edges of pocket across bottom of apron with right side of pocket facing wrong side of apron. Stitch across bottom and turn pocket up on apron.
3. Make ¼-inch hem on sides of apron, closing sides of pockets at the same time.
4. Gather top of apron to 16 inches.
5. Join two belt and tie pieces end to end.
6. Centering apron on joining in waistband, with wrong side of apron facing right side of band, adjust gathering and stitch.
7. Fold waistband and ties in half lengthwise, turn in ¼ inch all around, and topstitch, closing waistband over apron at the same time.
8. Make rows of stitching to divide pockets into 6 divisions as shown by dotted lines.

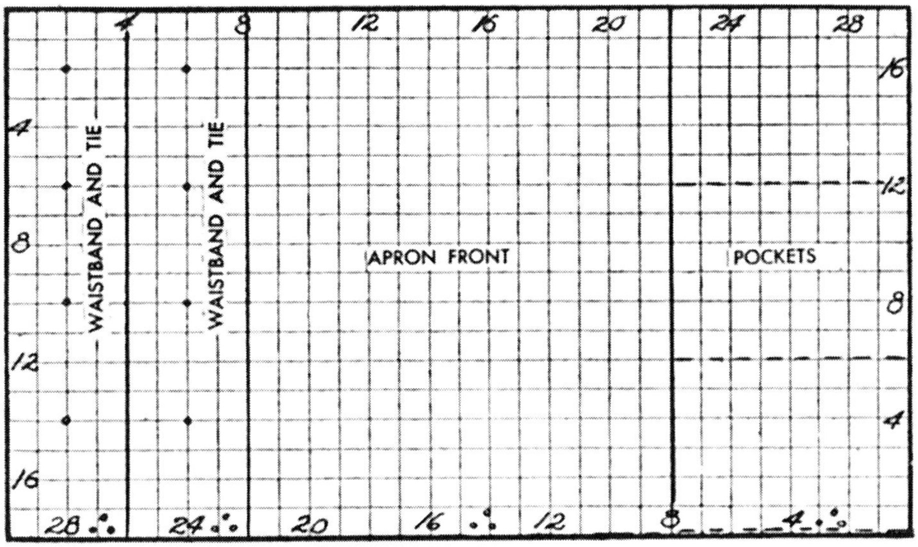

# Handkerchief Tea Apron

A dainty apron with a crocheted ruffle and ribbon ties.

**MATERIALS**

1 16-inch round, or 12-inch square handkerchief or doily; #30 mercerized crochet cotton; size 11 steel crochet hook; 1½ yards of 1½-inch ribbon.

**CROCHET AND ASSEMBLY**

Make a close row of single crochet (sc) around three sides of square apron, or to within last 5 inches on round. Turn.* Chain (ch) 5, skip 1 sc, sc in next sc. Repeat from * around ending with slip stitch (sl st) in last sc. Turn.

*For round apron only:* sl st to top of first loop, diminishing 1 loop each row.

*For square apron only:* ch 5, sc in top of first loop.

*For both aprons:* Continue with ch 5 loops for 3 inches. Now make ch 6 loops to within 3 inches of end of row. Finish row with ch 5 loops. Continue in this fashion for 10 rows, increasing 1 ch in each loop of each succeeding row except for first and last 3 inches of row which are always worked in ch 5 loops.

Turn in 1½ inches unruffled side of apron and hem down by hand, forming casing for ribbon. Run ribbon through casing.

# Patchwork Apron

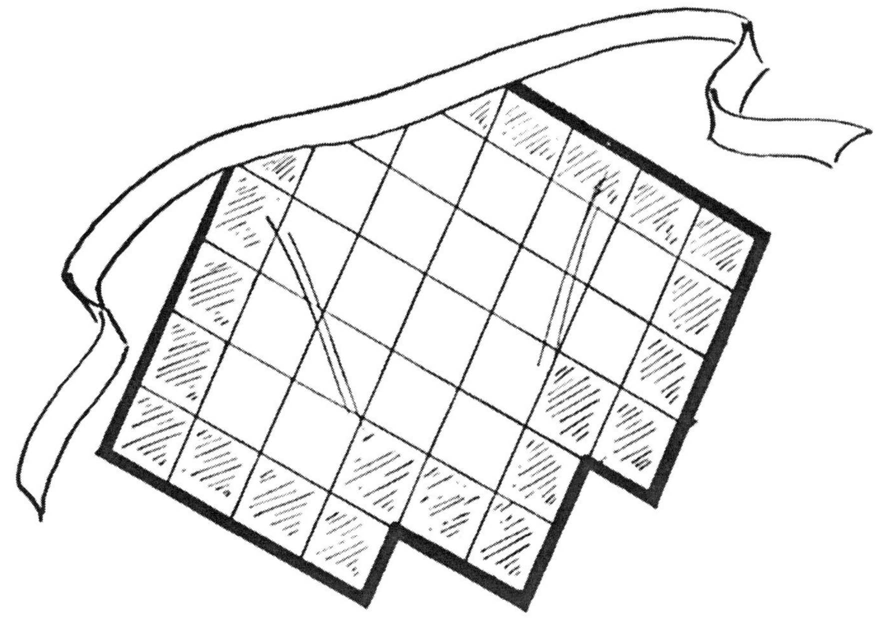

This gay apron utilizes scraps from the sewing basket, which may be arranged to produce a great many interesting effects, of light and dark patches, or plain and figured ones.

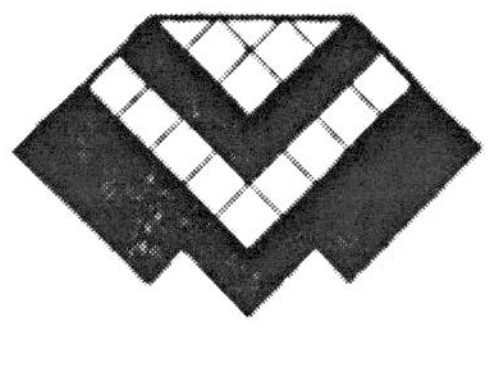

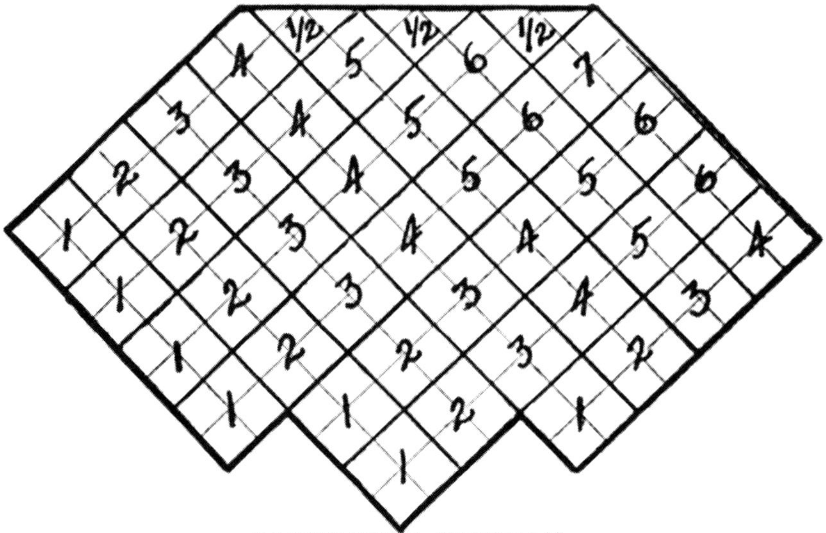


PATCHWORK DIAGRAM

Note: Each Small Square = 2 Inches

**MATERIALS**

Fabric scraps, assorted as desired; 2½ yards bias binding.

**CUTTING**

For a durable pattern, cut a 3½-inch square of cardboard and reinforce the edges with Scotch tape to prevent wear. On the wrong side of fabric, and straight of goods, draw around pattern with pencil, making 38 square patches and 3 triangular half patches. Cut a piece 2 yards long and 3¼ inches wide for ties and waistband. (This may be pieced.)

**SEWING**

1. Using ¼-inch seams, stitch squares in strips as shown in numbered diagram, arranging colors as desired.
2. Join strips as shown and whip all seams.
3. Bind entire outside edge except top with bias binding.
4. With wrong side of apron facing right side of band, center and join apron to band.
5. Close bands and ties, turning in all raw edges and top-stitching.

# Necktie Apron

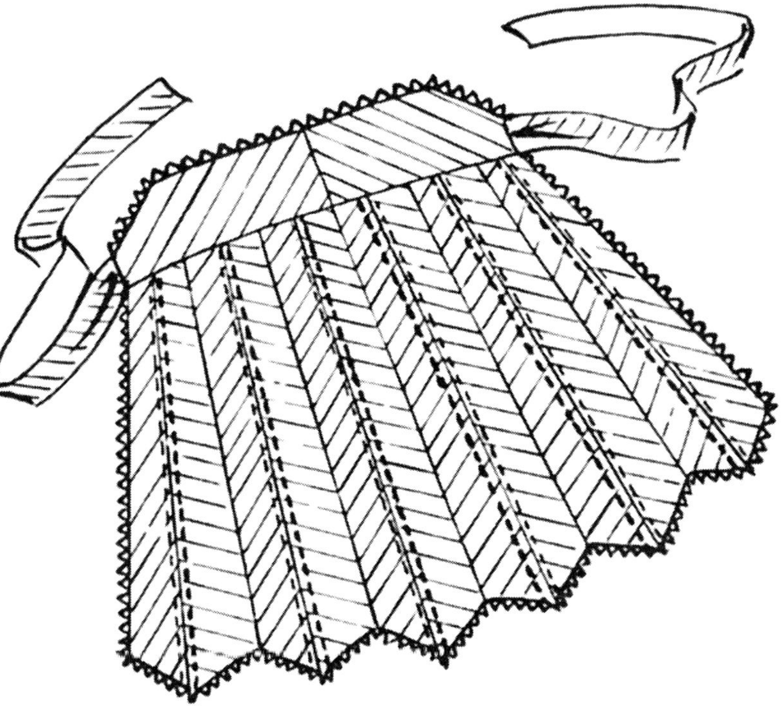

Always a favorite and sure-fire moneymaker at bazaars.

**MATERIALS**

1 yard of 36-inch vertically striped cotton fabric; 2½ yards of rickrack.

**CUTTING**

Use cutting layout, being sure to fold fabric on stripe or halfway between so that stripes will match in corresponding pieces. First cut bias panels measuring 3½ inches wide and 17 inches long (on short side). Taper sides as shown, starting with ⅔ inch on top.

**SEWING**

1. Join each pair of panels on longer side with ⅜-inch seam, matching stripes.
2. Join six pairs of panels, again matching stripes and forming points as illustrated in sketch.
3. Fold edges of longer joining seams and edgestitch to give accordion pleated effect.
4. Around sides and bottom of apron, make a ¼-inch turn-under and stitch rickrack under edge.
5. Seam waistband in center.
6. Hem ties. Attach facing to waistband, at the same time pleating ties and inserting at matching notches and inserting rickrack along dotted line. Turn facing.
7. Attach apron to lower edge of waistband facing, easing to fit. Turn under raw edge of waistband and stitch closed.
8. Iron this apron with topstitched seams creased to give a pleated effect.

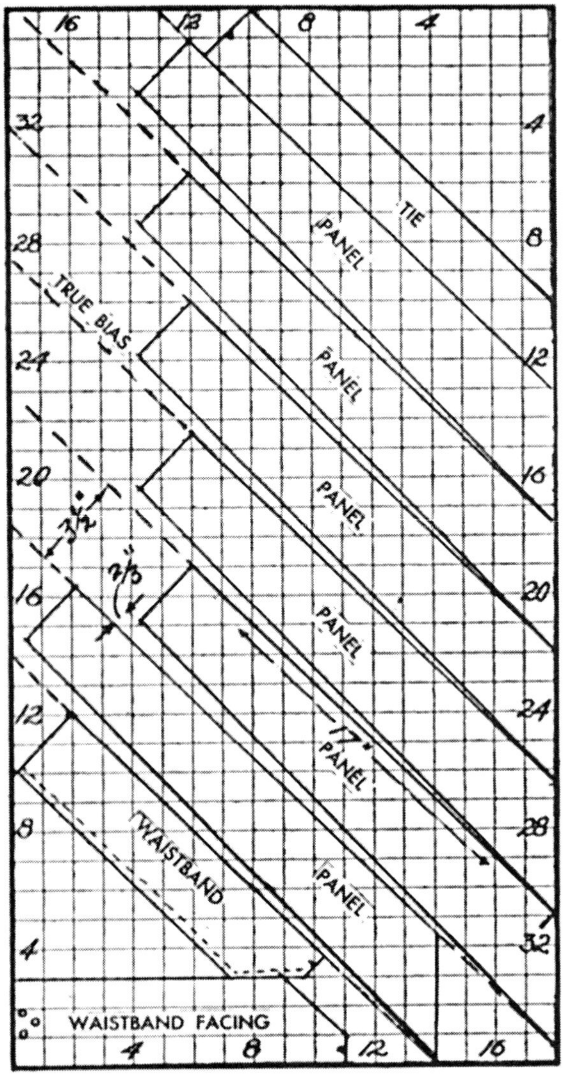

# Pocket Aprons

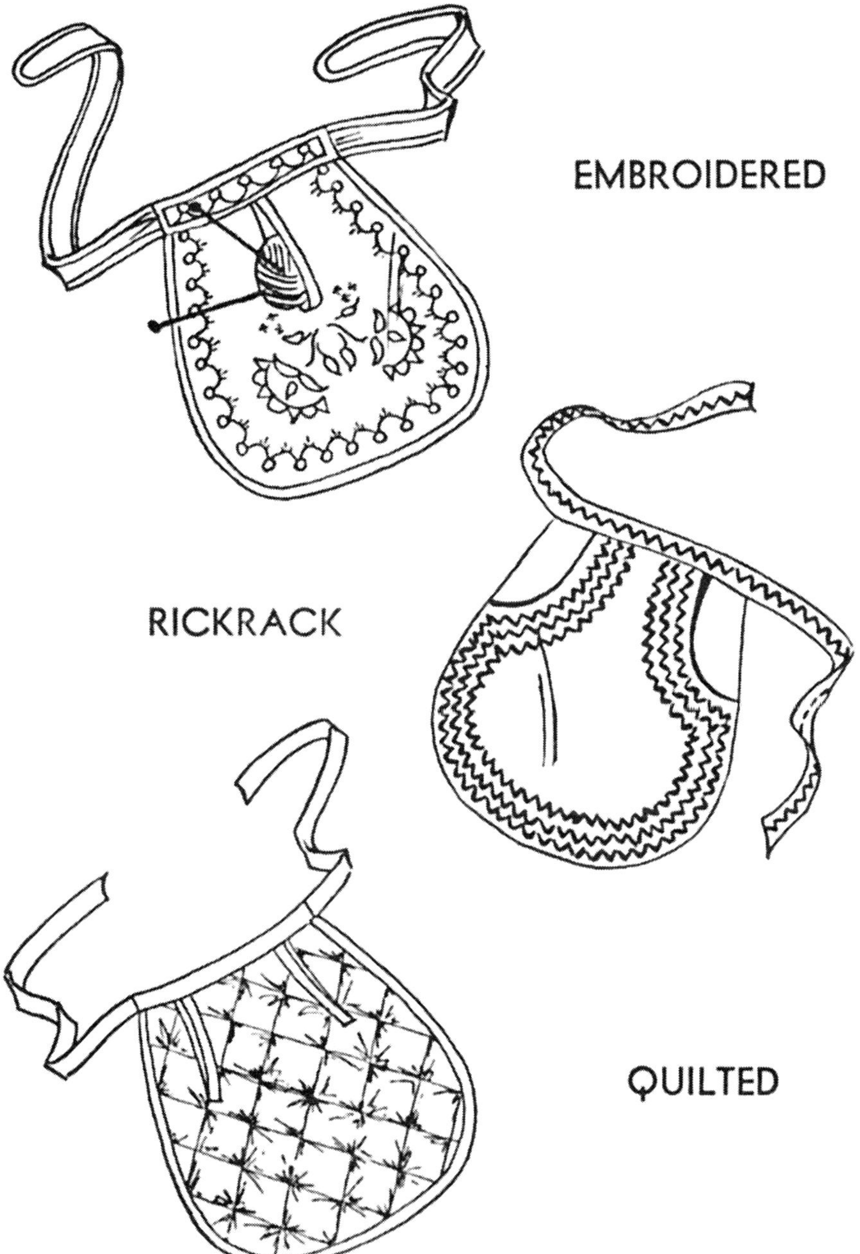


The pocket aprons shown here in their dressed-up version, to be used as needlework accessories, may also be made in sturdy fabric to hold clothespins.

# Embroidered-Pocket Apron

**MATERIALS**

32 inches of 36-inch linen; ⅜ yards of contrasting fabric for binding; six-strand embroidery floss or lightweight embroidery wool.

**CUTTING**

Use cutting layout placing back on center fold. Cut 7 yards of 1½-inch bias of contrasting fabric. (See method page 113.)

**EMBROIDERY**

Enlarge embroidery design (*see page 124*), and trace on front of apron and waistband, repeating design as shown in sketch. Embroider in colors indicated. For stitches, see page 124.

**SEWING**

1. After embroidery is completed, baste front and front lining of apron together around pocket opening and edges.
2. Bind pocket opening with bias (make all bindings ⅜ inch wide finished).

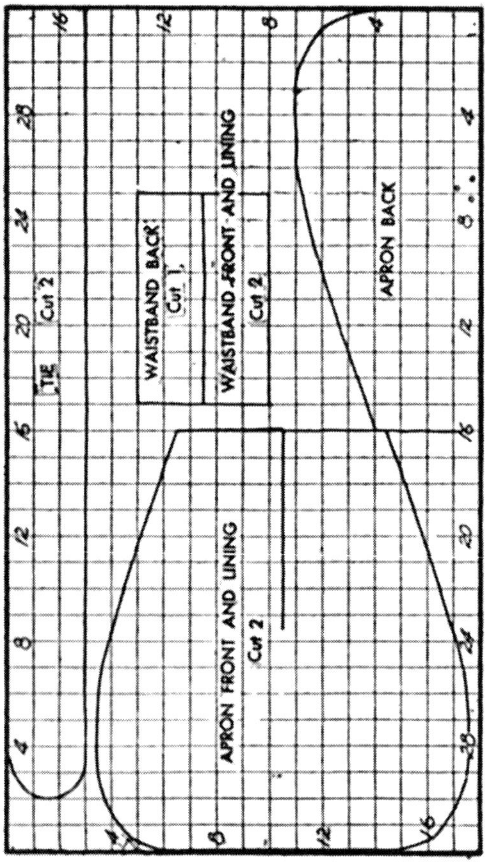

3. Baste front of apron to back, wrong sides together. Bind all three layers together around outer edge, except top.
4. Baste embroidered waistband to waistband lining and bind short ends.
5. Baste apron ties under each end of waistband, pleating in width of tie to exactly fit end of band. Blindstitch along line of binding on waistband.
6. Bind completely around ties and waistband.
7. Lap waistband over top of apron and blindstitch along line of binding. Face waistband with back piece, covering all raw edges.

## Quilted Apron with Two Slashed Pockets

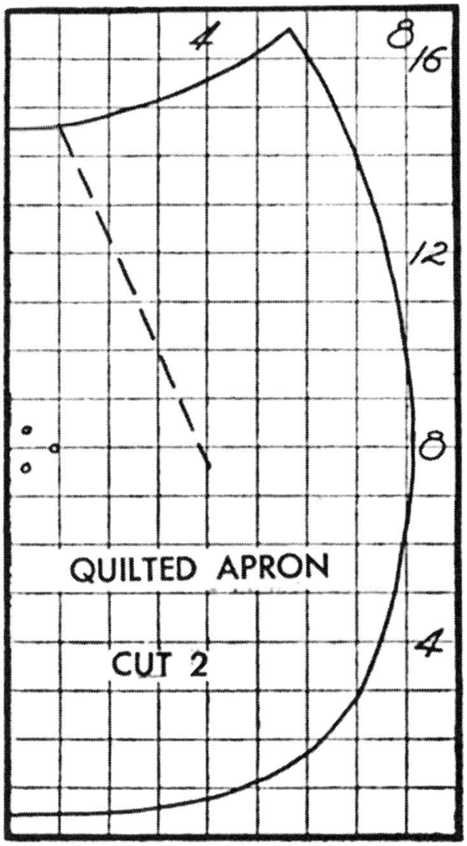


**MATERIALS**

½ yard of 36-inch quilted muslin *OR* quilted plastic *OR* ½ yard of sturdy unquilted fabric; 6½ yards of single-fold bias tape.

**Note.** If quilted fabric with only one side finished is used, ½ yard of plain material for lining will be necessary.

**CUTTING**

Cut two pieces as shown in diagram, laying pattern on fold. Slash one piece as shown by dotted line. If lining is to be used, cut two similar pieces of lining fabric.

**SEWING**

1. If apron is to be lined, baste front and back linings to front and back of apron, matching raw edges.
2. Bind slashes in front piece with bias tape.
3. Lay front and back of apron together, right side out, baste, and stitch once ¼ inch from edge for reinforcement all around, including top edge.
4. With bias tape, bind entire outer edge except top.
5. Double remaining bias tape at midpoint and edgestitch together on one side, turning in raw ends, thus forming waistband and ties ½ inch wide.
6. Insert top edge of apron between edges of waistband centering apron. Stitch apron to back of band.
7. Topstitch entire length of ties and waistband.

## Rickrack Pocket Apron

**MATERIALS**

20 inches of 36-inch fabric; 6 yards of rickrack; 2 yards of bias tape.

**CUTTING**

**Note.** Apron is cut cross-wise of material with fabric folded.

Use cutting layout, cutting away front piece of apron on dot and dash lines to form pockets.

1. Apply 3 rows of rickrack as shown by dotted lines to front apron piece. You may use three contrasting colors or all of the same color. *See page 125*. Face pocket edges with bias facing.
2. Lay both pieces of apron together, *both* right sides up. Baste lower edges together from X to X and top edges together from Y to Y on diagram. Face entire edge of apron except top with bias facing.
3. Join tie ends to ends of waistband piece, matching notches. Center apron on waistband with back of apron facing front side of band, and stitch.
4. Fold waistband and ties, turning in ¼ inch all around, and topstitch completely around ties and waistband. Trim waistband with one row of rickrack as shown.

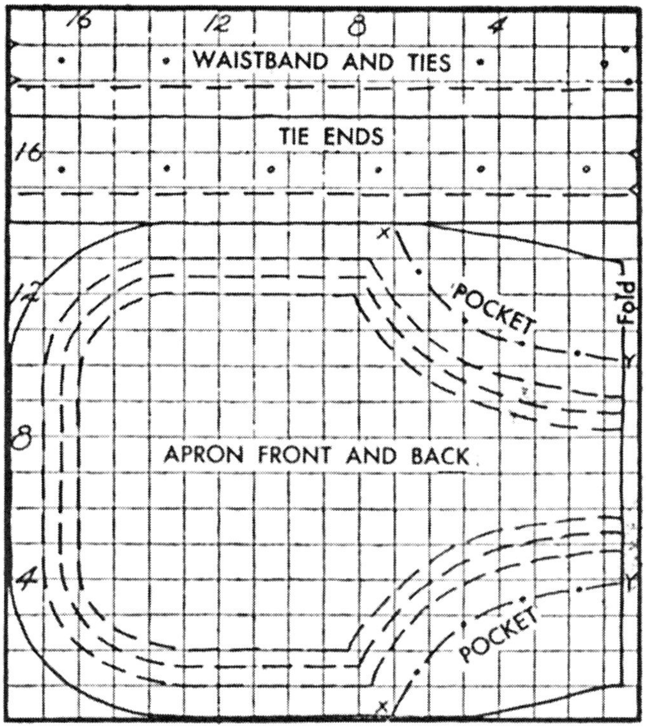

# Gardening Apron with Kneeling Flap

Kneeling flap fits neatly under the knees when needed and folds upward and snaps into place when not in use. Pockets and tool straps complete this apron's convenience. A leather belt, which buckles in back passes through a casing at apron top.

**MATERIALS**

1 yard of 36-inch waterproof canvas; a leather belt; 5 grip fasteners.

**CUTTING**

Cut apron on center fold, as shown in layout. Open out remaining material and divide in center. One half makes the kneeling flap. Cut the pocket piece and top facing from the other half.

**SEWING**

1. With right sides together, join apron and facing along top edge.

2. Make 1½-inch hem in one long edge of kneeling flap and a small hem in each side.
3. Open facing seam and make a ¼-inch hem in sides of facing, and in sides, and bottom of apron, at the same time centering and inserting raw edge of kneeling flap under lower hem with right side of flap facing wrong side of apron.

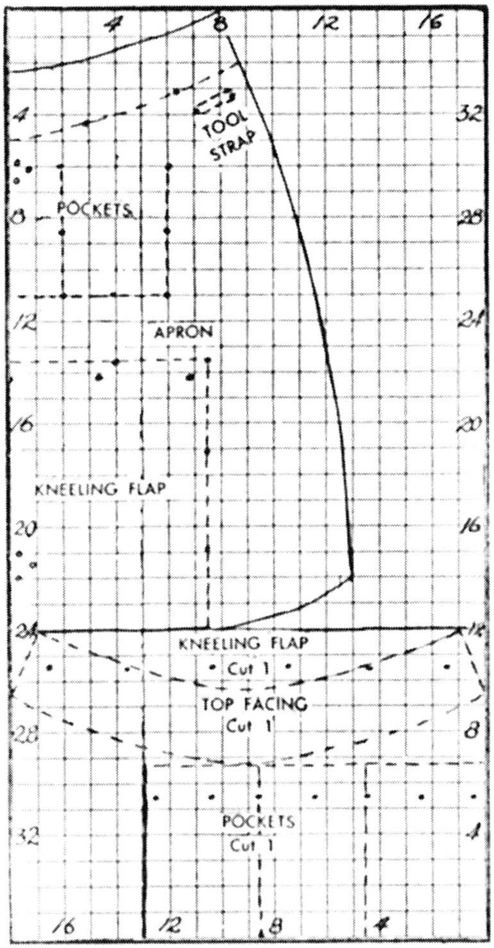


4. Fold flap outward, stitch again at fold of hem. Secure top to apron with five grip fasteners, spaced evenly.
5. Fold down facing and topstitch. Also stitch top edge of facing.
6. Make 1-inch hem in one long edge of pocket piece. Turn under ¼ inch on remaining raw edges and topstitch in position shown. Topstitch lines dividing piece into 3 pockets.
7. Cut 2 small strips 1 inch wide by 3½ inches long for tool straps. Fold over ⅓ inch from each side and stitch on each edge, and in center. Turn under ends and stitch in position shown.

# Split Apron for Gardening

*(To Wear Over Slacks)*

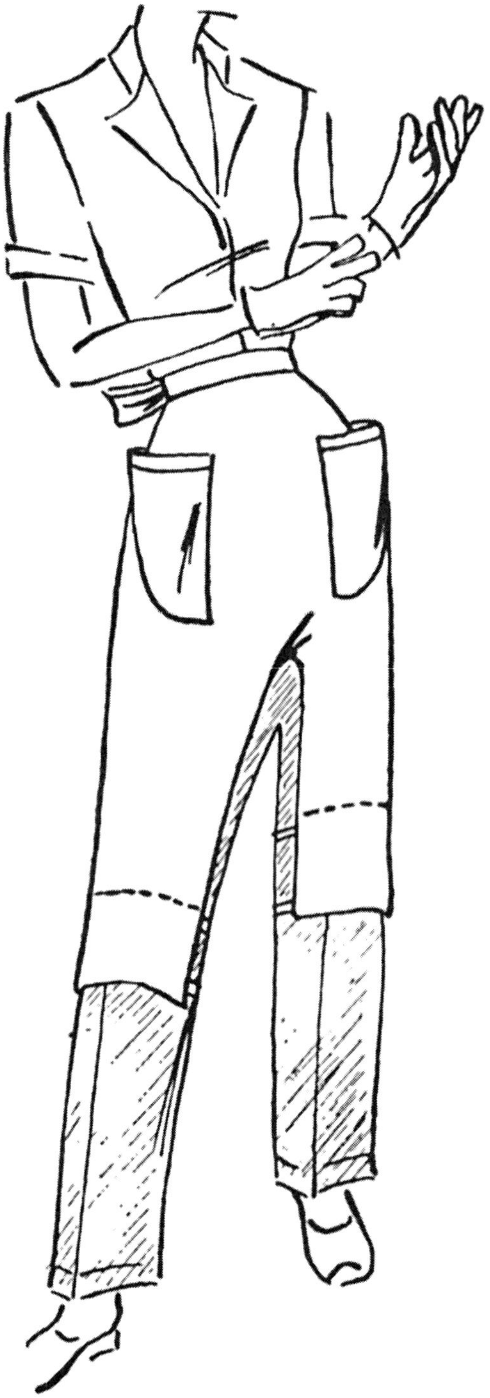

For gardening or painting floors, you'll find that this apron with knee pads pays real dividends.

**MATERIALS**

42 inches of 36-inch denim or other sturdy fabric; 3½ yards of ½-inch twill tape; 11 inches of 36-inch plastic material; small amount of cotton wadding.

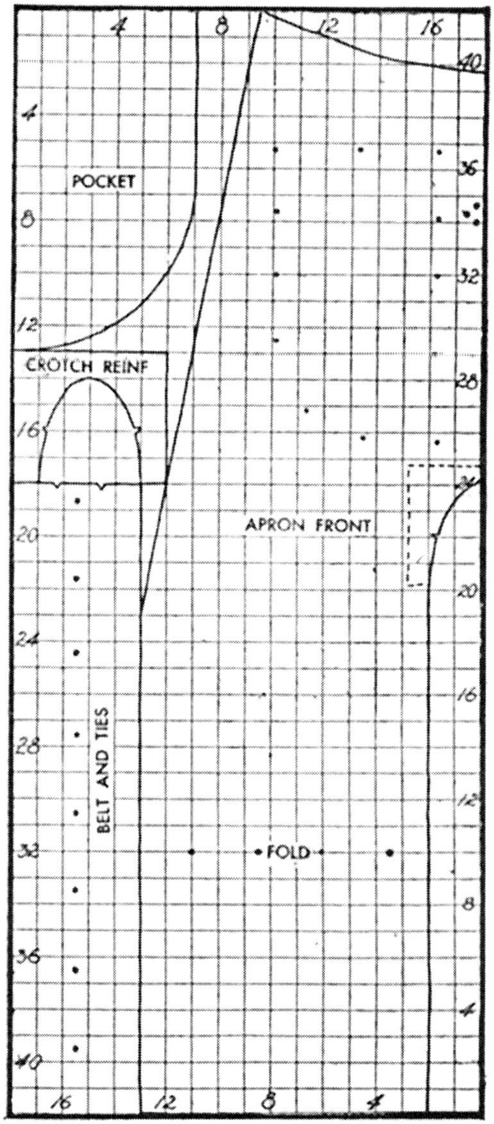


**CUTTING**

Follow cutting layout, placing apron on center fold.

**SEWING**

1. Place crotch reinforcement facing apron, with right sides together and notches matching, and stitch ½ inch from curved edge. Clip and turn.
2. Make a 1-inch hem at tops of pockets and, turning in raw edges, topstitch to apron as shown by dots. If desired, pockets may be trimmed across top with decorative woven tape.

3. Make ½-inch hem at bottom of legs. Fold legs toward front on dotted lines, stitch on sides and turn, forming pockets on wrong side at knees.
4. Hem outer edges of apron above knee pockets, and inner edges between crotch facing and knee pockets. Turn in raw edges of crotch facing ¼ inch and topstitch all around.
5. Join belt pieces end to end. Center top of apron on belt joining with wrong side of apron facing right side of belt and stitch.
6. Fold entire belt and tie pieces, turning in ¼ inch on all raw edges, and topstitch closed.
7. Cut twill tape in 8 equal pieces. Attach piece at top and bottom of each side of knee pockets, turning under raw end and stitching back and forth several times. These tapes tie behind the knees, holding pads in place.
8. Make knee pads of plastic. Cut 2 pieces of plastic 18 by 11 inches. Fold crosswise, stitch sides, and turn. Fill with wadding to about a one-inch thickness, close and stitch. Stitch twice in each direction to hold wadding in place. Insert in knee pockets.

# Barbecue Sets for the Family

*(Apron, Mitt, and Hat)*

Make sets for all the members of the family, to dress them up for back-yard picnics. Unbleached muslin or faded blue denim are suggested for the apron and mitt; white percale for the hat.

*For embroidery design see pages 118 and 119.*

**Apron and Mitt**

**MATERIALS**

*For men:* 40 inches of 36-inch fabric; 4½ yards of double-fold bias tape.

*For women:* 34 inches of 36-inch fabric; 4 yards of double-fold bias tape.

*For children:* 30 inches of 36-inch fabric; 3½ yards of double-fold bias tape.

*In addition, for each mitt:* 12 inches of 36-inch flannelette; 1⅛ yards of binding; 8 inches of elastic.

**CUTTING**

Use cutting layout. Note dotted lines marked *small, medium, large* for the different sizes of apron. Dotted line indicates small size for mitt.

**SEWING**

**Apron**

1. Bind entire outside edge of apron.
2. Join two pieces of neck strap end to end. Fold lengthwise, turn in both edges, topstitch closed.
3. Fold apron strings and stitch in same manner.
4. Attach ends of neck strap to top corners of apron, adjusting length in smaller sizes and stitching securely.
5. Attach apron strings to back corners in the same manner.
6. Embroider in suitable colors, or use iron-on transfer.

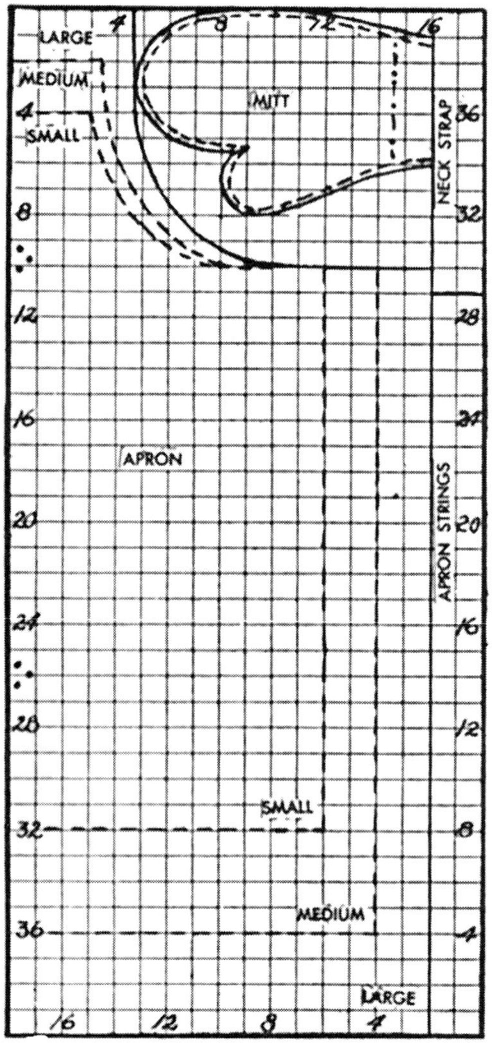

### Mitt

1. Lay mitt pieces on folded flannelette. Cut two layers for lining and interlining of front and same for back.
2. Baste one lining, one interlining and one mitt piece together, for the front, and one similar set for the back.
3. Bind both front and back across wrist edge.
4. Make two lines of stitching on back side of mitt ⅜ inches apart (see dot and dash line). Which is the back of mitt is determined of course by whether you want a right or a left mitt. Run elastic in casing thus formed, drawing up to 3 inches and securing at both ends.
5. Lay front and back of mitt together, flannel sides facing, stitch and bind, making additional 2-inch loop on thumb side.

## BARBECUE HAT

### MATERIALS

25 inches of 36-inch percale; 9 by 24¾ inches of muslin for interlining.

### CUTTING

Cut a circle 25 inches in diameter for hat top. To draw a circle, tie string to pencil and place pin through string 12½ inches from pencil. Draw with pencil at string length pivoting around pin. Cut piece 9 inches wide and 24¾ inches long for hatband. Cut similar piece of muslin for interlining.

### SEWING

1. Baste interlining to hatband around all sides.
2. Join short sides of hatband, forming circle.
3. Gather hat top around edge and pin to hatband with right sides together. Distribute gathers evenly and stitch.
4. Fold hatband under and whip edge, covering gathers.

# French Bartender's Apron

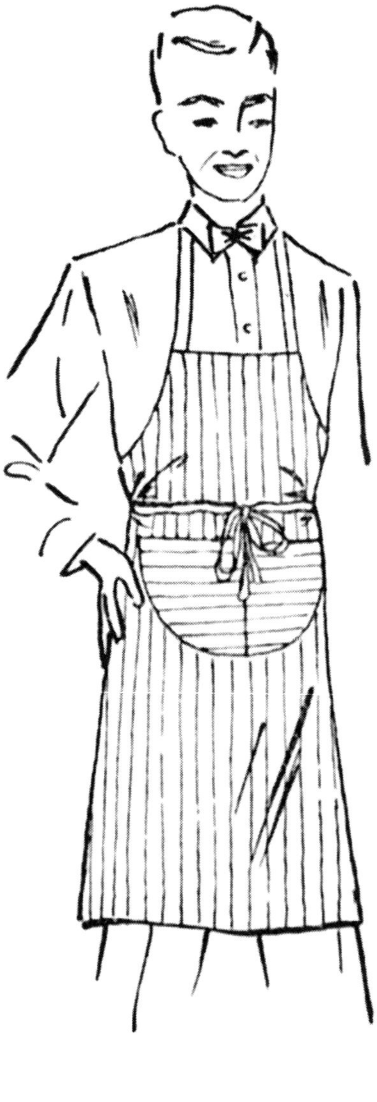

This picturesque apron worn by the bistro keeper in France has extra thickness to protect the gentleman's front. The ties are long ones that come around and tie in front.

**MATERIALS**

32 inches of 36-inch striped ticking.

**CUTTING**

Use cutting fabric layout on folded fabric.

SEWING

1. Join pocket pieces, matching notches and stripes. Make a small hem on the straight side.
2. Topstitch pocket, folding under raw edges, in place around curved edge, as shown by dots and stitch up and down on each side of center seam.
3. Sew two pieces of neck strap together end to end. Turn in edges and topstitch closed. Also topstitch on folded edge.
4. Make apron strings in the same manner.
5. Make a small hem around entire apron, slipping ends of neck strap under hem at Y on diagram and apron strings under hem at X on diagram.
6. Turn neck strap and apron strings outward and reinforce by stitching several times back and forth at edges of apron.

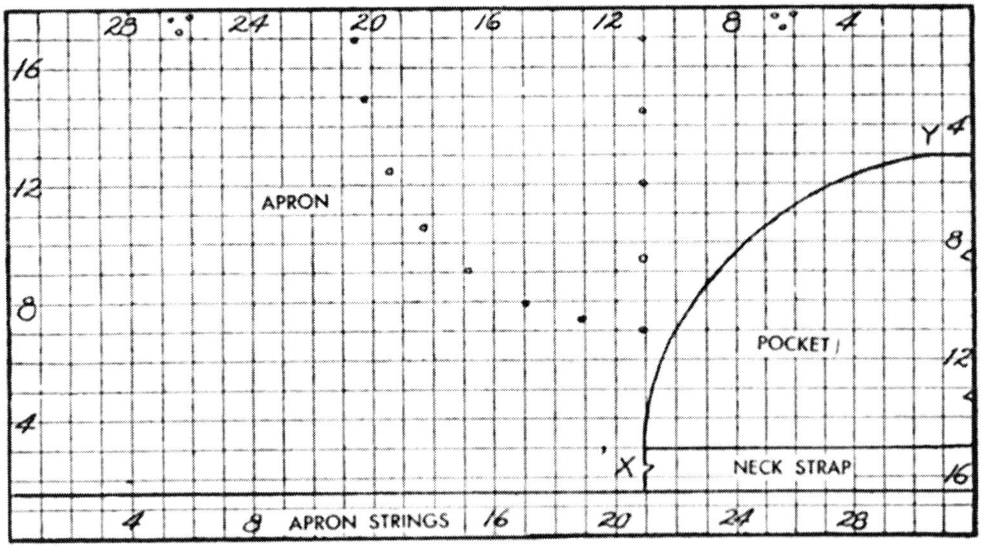

# Sportsman's Apron

It seems that a man, whether at home washing dishes, or cleaning fish by a stream, instinctively prefers a towel tucked in his belt to any shape or form of apron. So put a sinker on each upper corner of a plain sugar sack dish towel, which makes for easier tucking, and let him have his way. We'll wager this is one apron he will tuck in his fishing kit or pack alongside his rabbit-skinning knife.

**MATERIALS**

1 yard unbleached muslin *OR* a 36-inch square sugar sack; 2 2-inch drapery weights or flat sinkers.

**SEWING**

1. Make a small hem on all 4 sides of the sugar sack or muslin.
2. Put top corners through holes in weights and sew down about 1 inch of corner securely.

## Wood-Carrying Apron

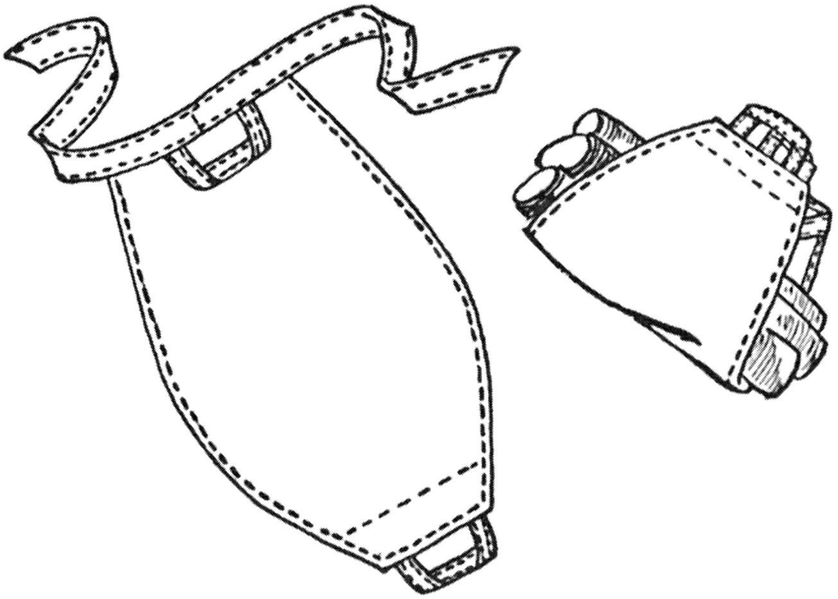

Tie the apron around your waist and hold by the handle at the bottom to form a sling for logs, or carry by both handles, like a bag.

**MATERIALS**

32 inches of 36-inch heavy denim.

**CUTTING**

Follow cutting layout.

**SEWING**

**Note.** Use large stitch and heavy matching or contrasting thread.

1. Fold handles as indicated, turn in raw edges on long sides, and topstitch closed. Stitch close to edge on folded side.

2. Piece bottom facing as indicated by notches.
3. With right sides of fabric together, join facing to lower end of apron, at the same time inserting between the facing and apron, from underneath, the two ends of handle, evenly spaced. Be careful not to twist. Stitch on sides and end, beginning and ending on sides ½ inch from wide edge of facing. Reinforce end with several rows of stitching. Turn facing.
4. Make small hems in sides of apron.
5. Turn in raw edge of facing and topstitch closed, continuing stitching around entire edge of facing.
6. Join belt pieces, end to end as indicated by the notches.
7. Center belt on apron top with wrong side of apron facing right side of belt. Stitch in place, at the same time inserting remaining handle ends, spaced the same as lower handle and reinforcing with several rows of stitching.
8. Close belt and ties, at the same time turning in all raw edges, and topstitch around both sides and ends.

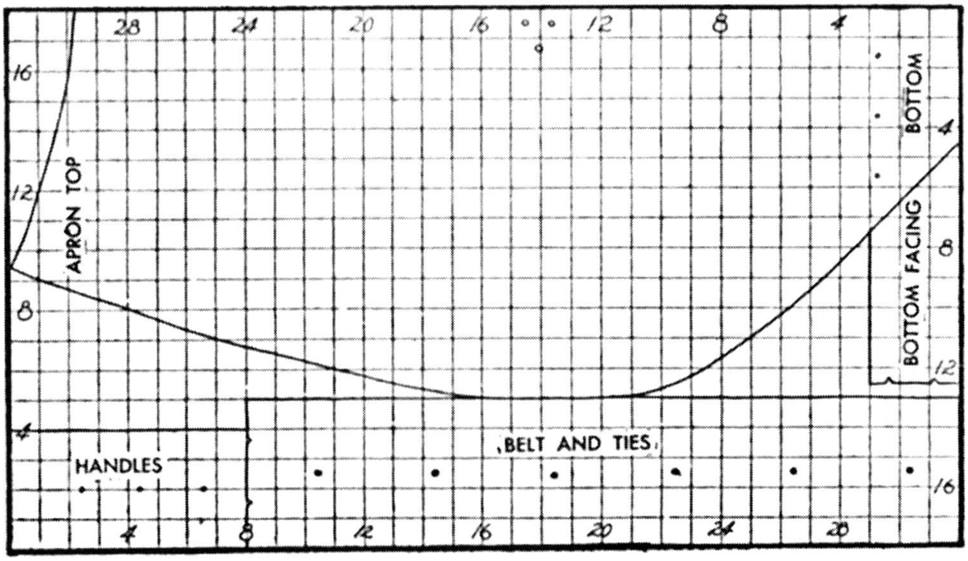

# Mend-While-You-Iron Apron

*(One Size)*

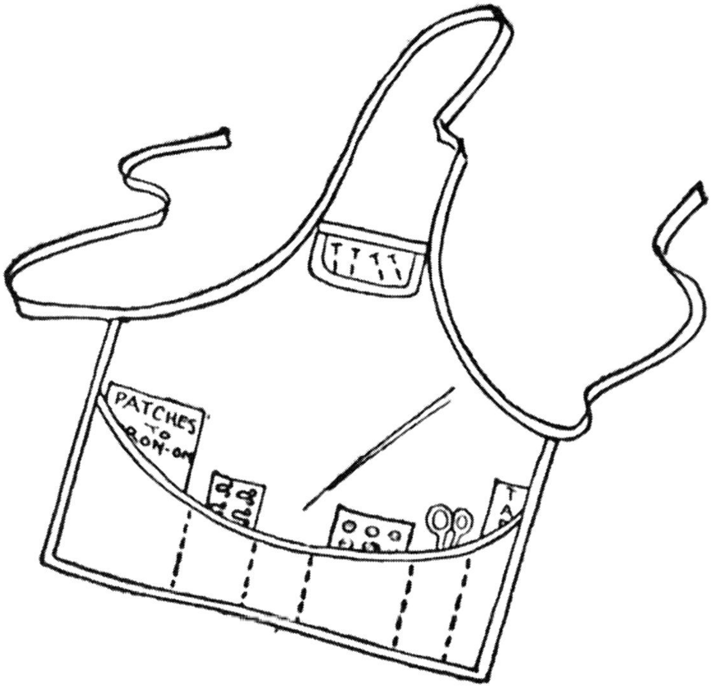


Many tiny repairs such as replacing a button, or mending a torn buttonhole can be made most easily at the time the garment is being ironed. Then, linen and children's overalls can be patched with iron-on tape or fabric. Assemble all the necessary tools in this handy apron to wear while you iron.

**MATERIALS**

⅝ of a yard of denim, 24 inches wide; 6 yards of extra width bias binding.

*Accessories:* iron-on tape; iron-on patches; snaps, hooks and eyes, buttons; light and dark thread; blunt-pointed scissors; pins and needles.

**CUTTING**

Use cutting layout shown.

**SEWING**

1. Bind curved edges of pocket piece and one long end and sides of pin holder.
2. Baste raw edges of pin holder pieces to top of apron and bind edge.
3. Place pocket piece across bottom of apron and baste on three straight sides.
4. Bind bottom of apron beginning at point A and ending at the corresponding point on the other side.
5. Fold and stitch closed 27 inches of tape and without cutting tape, proceed to bind curved side of apron; stitch closed another 27 inches for neck, bind remaining curved side; and finally stitch closed 27 more inches of tape for the other tie.
6. Make vertical lines of stitching as shown by dotted lines to divide pocket for accessories.

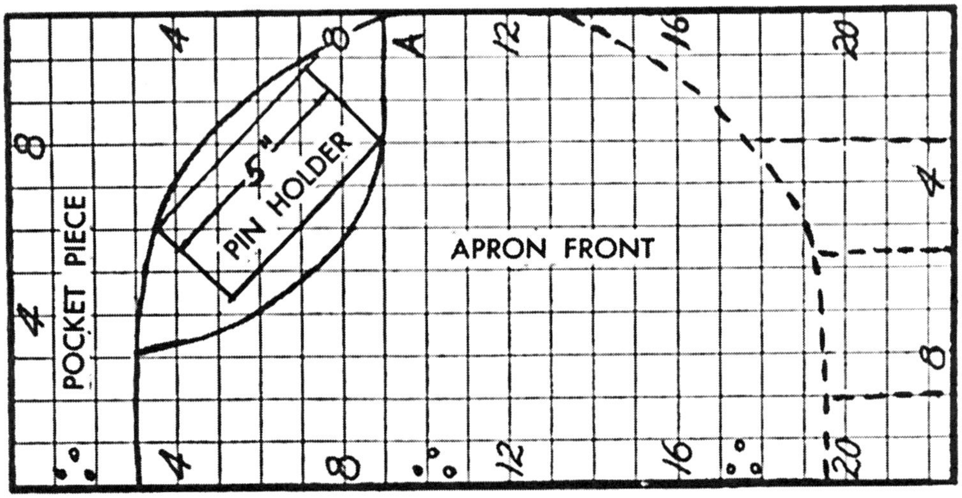

# Dressmaking Apron

Keep this apron where you sew and you'll always be equipped. Expert seamstresses recommend using green sateen for a work apron, as it provides a restful background.

**MATERIALS**

Fabric for any basic apron pattern you choose; 1 yard of twill tape; washable tape measure; scissors; pincushion; button.

**SEWING**

1. Use tape measure as trimming, being sure not to stretch or pucker it in stitching.
2. Cut six-inch length of twill tape and fold it in half. Secure fold to one side of pincushion. Insert ends under waistband of apron on left side.
3. Pass remainder of tape through handles of scissors and secure both ends under waistband on right side of center.
4. Make a small pocket 1½ inches square with button or snap closing, to hold thimble.

# Mending-Bag Apron

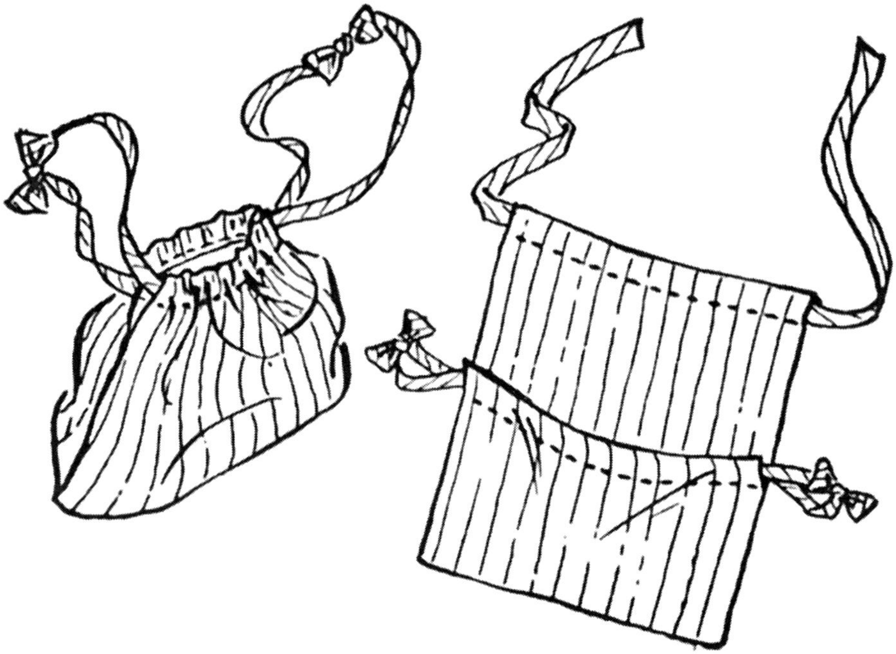

This mending-bag apron has two pockets, one to keep your mending in, the other for supplies and for tucking the apron top into when not in use.

**MATERIALS**

1 yard of 36-chintz or cretonne *OR* 24 inches of fabric and 4½ yards of 1½-inch tape or cord for strings and ties.

**CUTTING**

**Note.** *Each square in this diagram equals 2 inches.*

Use cutting layout, omitting bias if ties and strings are not of self fabric.

**SEWING**

1. Turn under ¼ inch at bottom of apron piece, and with *wrong* sides of fabric together, lap half-way over bag piece and top-stitch to dotted line at middle.

2. Fold back lower half of bag so that right sides are facing and stitch up sides of bag and apron to point 3 inches from top of bag (marked by dots on diagram).
3. Clip to end of stitching and turn bag. You now have a bag with apron in center dividing it.
4. Hem sides of apron with small hem.
5. Hem each side of bag down to joining, folding in all raw edges, but not closing ends of hem. This is the casing for the bag strings.
6. Make casing of similar size in top of apron.
7. If strings and ties of self fabric are used, join 2½-inch wide bias strips into single long piece, fold, stitch, and turn. (See page 113.) Cut 2 lengths 1¼ yards long for bag strings, and 1 length 2 yards long for apron ties.
8. Using a safety pin as bodkin, thread into place and tie strings near ends.

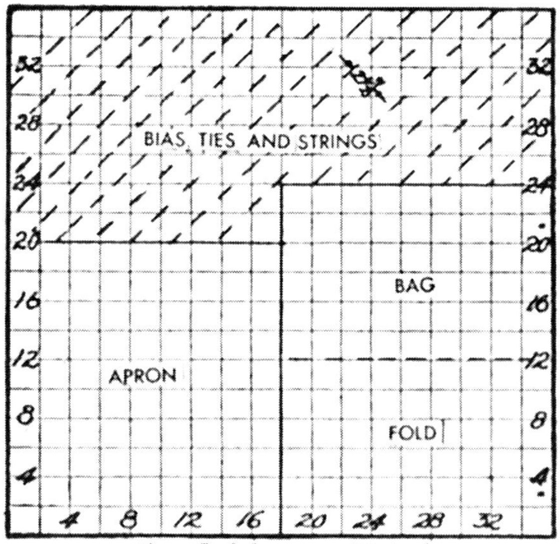

Note: Each Square = 2 Inches

# Hair-Washing Apron

Made of terry cloth (with a snug neckline to deter any dribbles), the apron itself may be used as a drying towel after the shampoo.

**MATERIALS**

1 yard of 36-inch terry cloth; cotton yarn for crochet or blanket stitch; 1 yard twill tape; 2 buttons.

**CUTTING**

Use cutting layout.

**SEWING**

1. Turn in ¼ inch on each end of neckband and fold in half lengthwise. Baste long edges together.
2. Beginning at center back of neck, turn in neck edge ½ inch

and topstitch over raw edges of neckband. Neckband should meet at back but not lap.

3. Stitch neckband ½ inch from top fold, forming casing. Whip back edges of neckband together up to beginning of casing.
4. Adjust waistband to fit and turn in ends, allowing a 2-inch lapover for buttons and buttonholes.

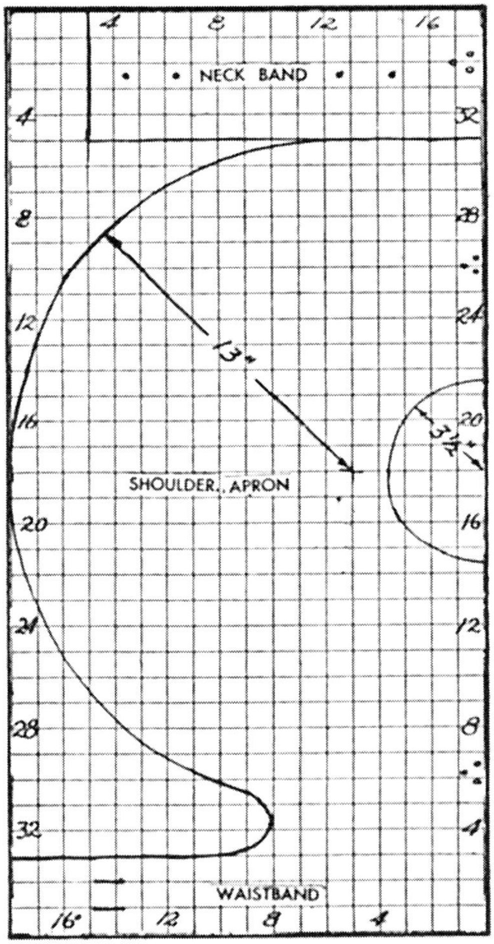


5. Turn in entire outer edge ¼ inch and stitch. Finish either with single crochet or buttonhole stitch.
6. Run twill tape through neck casing and secure at midpoint in front, with a few stitches to keep it from pulling out.
7. Make 2 buttonholes and place matching buttons on back of waistband.

# Vacuum-Cleaning Apron

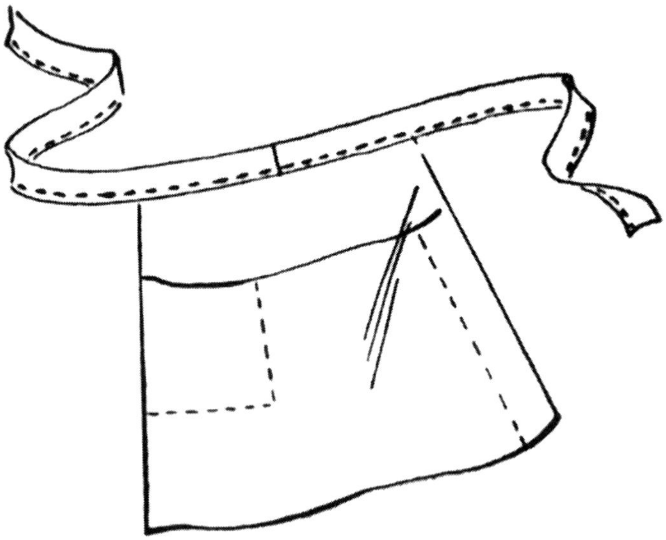

Wear this as an apron and have cleaning attachments at finger tips. When not in use, it serves as a tidy holder for the various parts.

**MATERIALS**

⅞ of a yard of 36-inch sailcloth or felt.

**CUTTING**

Use cutting layout.

**SEWING**

1. Make small hem in pocket edge as shown by dots.
2. Fold wrong side out, along line A-B and stitch sides of pocket. Turn pocket.
3. Clip seam at top of pocket and make a small hem along the remaining part of apron sides.
4. Make a division for radiator tool on left side of apron by

stitching along line C-D. Make a short division on the right side, stitching from E, around corner, to F.

5. Join band and tie pieces end to end.
6. Center joining on top of apron and stitch, with wrong side of apron facing the right side of band.
7. Turn in all raw edges and topstitch band and ties closed.

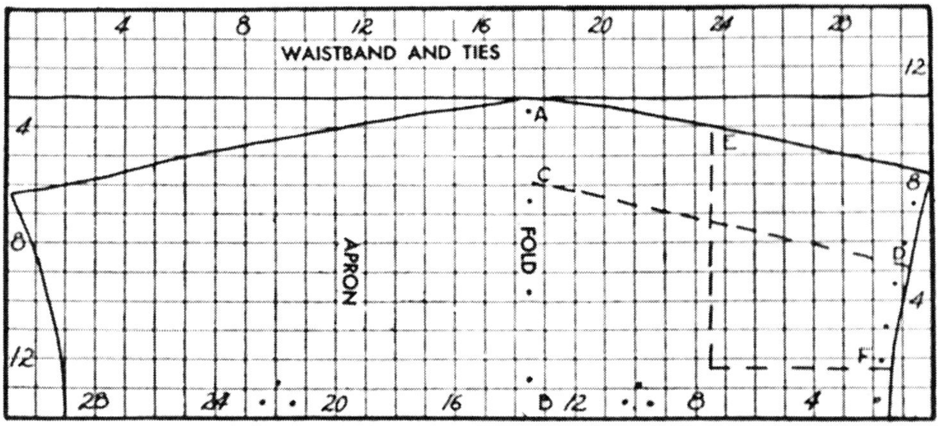

## Apron Accessories

Make these to match your favorite aprons.

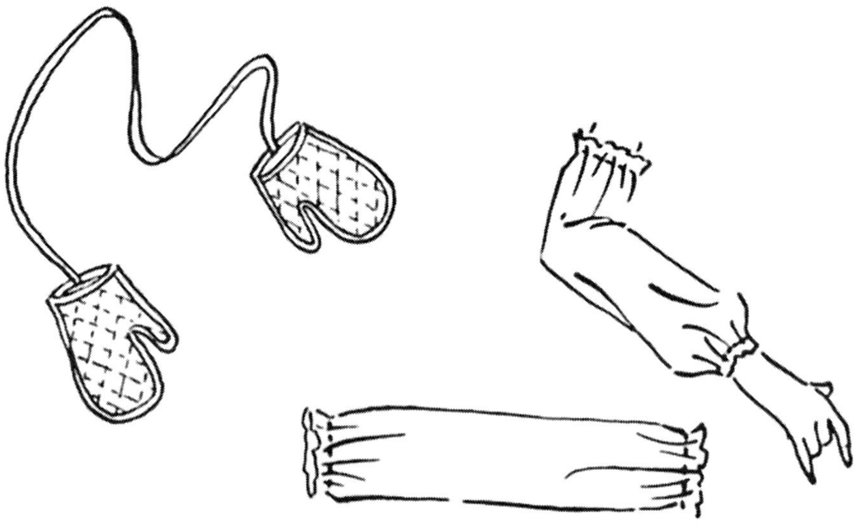

## Sleeve Guards

These keep your sleeves clean and also protect arms from heat.

**MATERIALS**

16 inches of 36-inch fabric; 1 yard of ¼-inch elastic.

**CUTTING**

Cut two pieces 16 by 18 inches.

**SEWING**

1. Fold pieces in middle of 18-inch side and seam on the 16-inch sides, forming sleeves.
2. Make a ½-inch hem for casing at top and bottom of each sleeve, leaving an opening.
3. Insert elastic through one casing to fit wrist and in other one to fit upper arm. Join ends of elastic and close casing.

## Quilted Potholder Mitts on Tape

When you're canning or baking, you'll find these mitts hanging right where you need them . . . a real help!

**MATERIALS**

½ yard of 36-inch outer fabric; 12 inches of 36-inch flannel or sailcloth for lining; 2½ yards of bias binding; 1½ yards of twill tape.

**CUTTING**

Using layout diagram as shown, cut 6 mitt-shaped pieces of outer fabric. Using lower part of diagram only, cut 4 pieces of lining fabric.

**SEWING**

1. Lay together, right sides out, 2 pieces of outer fabric with 2 lining pieces between them for palm of each mitt.
2. Quilt the 4 pieces together, stitching on dotted lines.
3. Lay quilted palms and back pieces together, right sides out and stitch ¼ inch from edge for reinforcement, leaving wrist open.

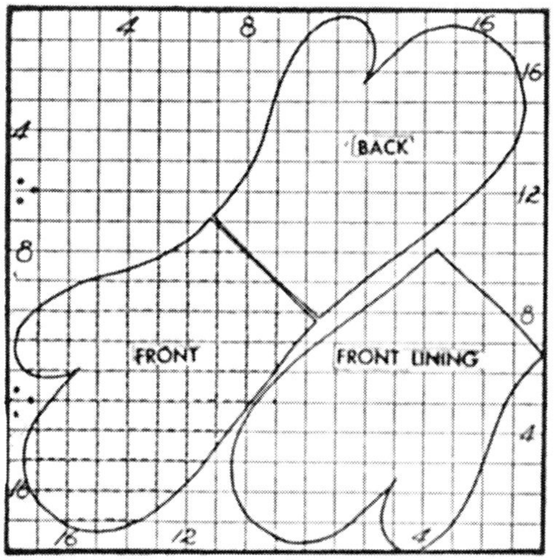


4. Bind outer edges just seamed with bias binding.
5. Bind around wrist edges.
6. Attach one end of twill tape to center back of each mitt.

# Potholders

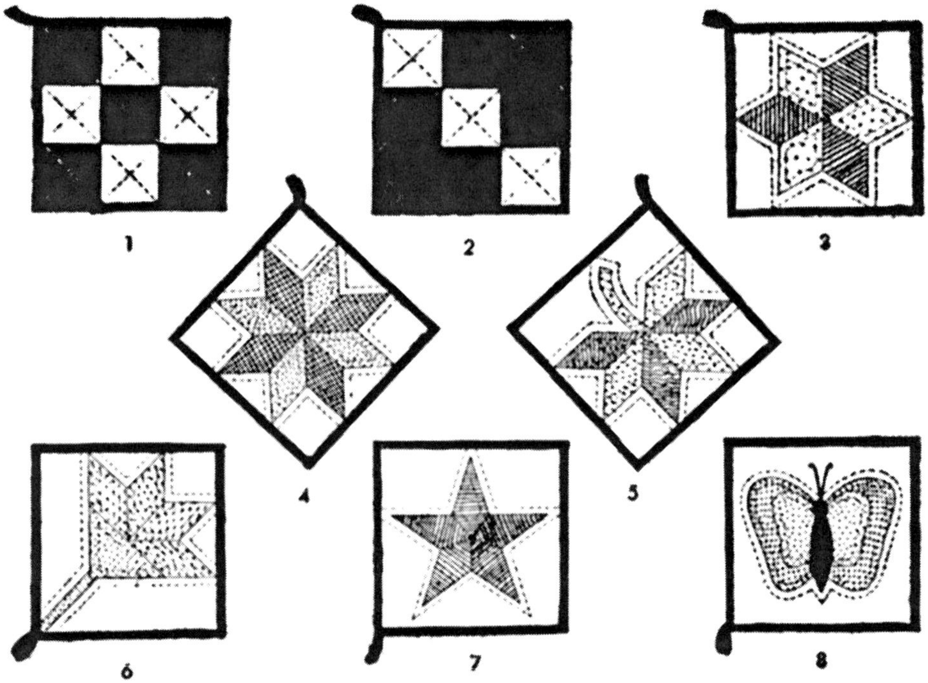

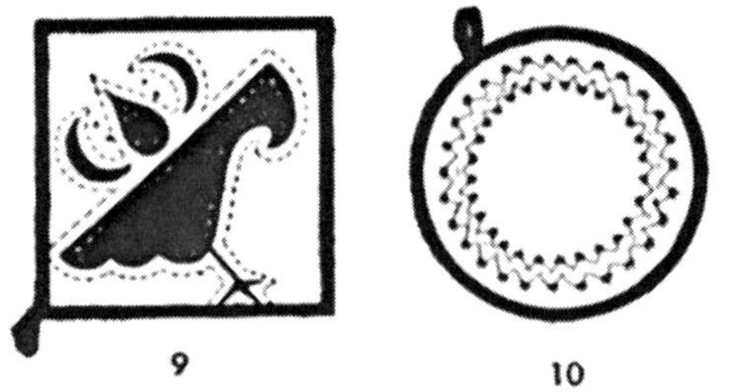

1. Nine Patch (pieced).
2. Nine Patch Variation (pieced).
3. Rising Star (pieced).
4. Eight Pointed Star (appliqué).
5. Peony (appliqué).
6. North Carolina Lily (appliqué).
7. Five Pointed Star (appliqué).
8. Butterfly (appliqué).
9. Bird (appliqué and embroidery).
10. Round (rickrack and embroidery).

**MATERIALS**

*Front and back:* scraps of colorfast, washable cotton. *Interlining:* cotton batting, flannelette, or sailcloth. *Edge:* bias binding.

**GENERAL DIRECTIONS**

Add ¼-inch seam allowance on all sides of patterns for individual pieces shown on page 110. If flannelette or sailcloth is used, make three layers of interlining in addition to front and back. If cotton batting or flannelette is used, the holder should be quilted either by hand or machine. Sail canvas makes a flat holder which need not be quilted. If potholder is to be quilted, make the back of plain material. Quilting lines may follow the shape of the decoration or produce a design of their own, and are done through all layers of holder. Dotted lines on full-sized patterns suggest how quilting may be done. Holders are finished with bias binding around edge and the loop is made by doubling 3-inch piece of bias.

**1 and 2**

Cut pieces by pattern A. Arrange patches as shown in sketches and piece together with ¼-inch seams. Quilt as shown.

**3**

Cut pieces by pattern B. Piece together and quilt, following arrangement in sketch.

**4, 5, and 6**

Use 6½-inch muslin square as base. Cut pieces by pattern C. Mark center lines on base and appliqué pieces, alternating fabrics as shown in sketches. Quilt as shown by dotted lines and also the same distance around outside of design. For 5 and 6, cut flower stems of bias. For 6 cut triangle for base of flower to fit as shown.

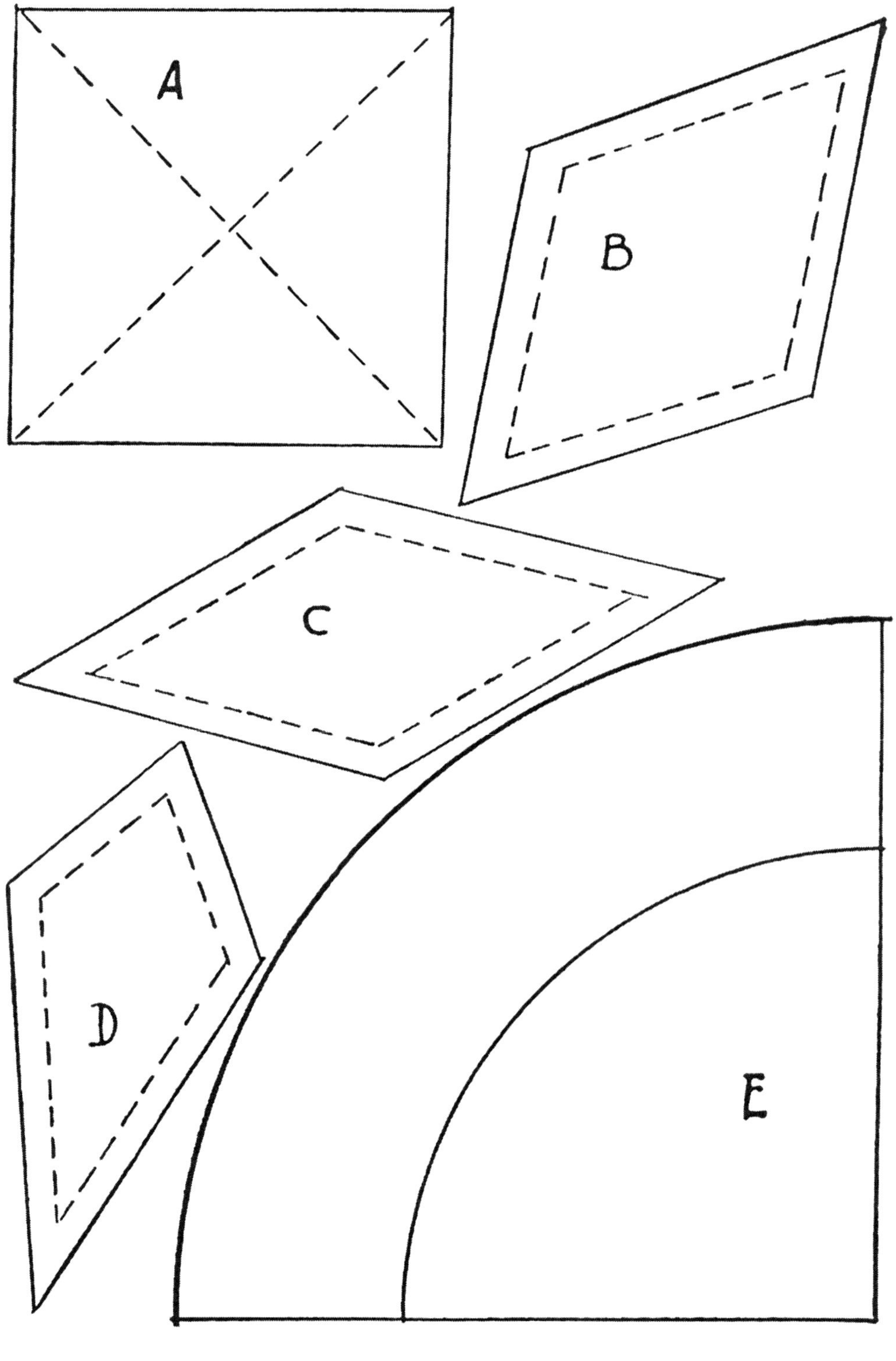
A
B
C
D
E

**7**

Cut pieces by pattern D. Use 6½-inch muslin square as base. Find center point of base. If *short, wide points* are arranged around center, they make a 5-pointed star as shown in sketch. 10 pieces of pattern D, with *long points* placed at center will make a 10-pointed, flowerlike design. Quilt ¼ inch inside each piece of star.

**8**

Use pattern shown on page 121, adding ¼ inch seam allowance all around for wings of butterfly. Appliqué pieces to 6½-inch square muslin base. Shape and appliqué pieces for body and head. Embroider feelers. Quilt ¼-inch inside and outside of outlines.

**9**

Enlarge diagram on page 118 and cut pattern, adding ¼ inch seam allowance all around. Dots, leg and eye are embroidered. Quilt ¼ inch inside and around outline of bird and flower.

**10**

Cut circle by pattern E. (¼ pattern shown). No seam allowance is necessary. Assemble holder. Quilt on dotted line. Apply rick-rack, centering it over quilting. (*See stitch diagram on page 125.*) Do not allow embroidery stitches to come through to back.

**FULL-SIZED DIAGRAMS (OPPOSITE)**

A. Single block of 9-patch. B. Single piece of rising star. C. Single piece of 8-pointed star. D. Single piece of 5-pointed star. E. ¼ pattern for round potholder.

# Sewing Tricks for Apron Makers

**HAND-SEWN HEMS**

Hems are easier to finish if the first turn is machine-stitched very close to the edge. Hand-hemming is then done with tiny vertical stitches about ½ inch apart, with an extra stitch in the turned edge only, every 4 or 5 stitches.

**USE OF MACHINE HEMMER**

Cut a small triangle, about $\frac{3}{16}$ inch wide, off corner to be started through hemmer. This makes feeding into the folder easier. Push corner in far enough so that needle of machine catches it. Holding free end of thread and pulling slightly, start to stitch. Hold fabric in front of foot and slightly to the left with the right thumb and forefinger and bend edge slightly to the approximate depth of hem. Hemmer folder will take care of the turn-under. It may take practice to get used to your particular hemmer, as hemmers vary in adjustment. The hem folds more evenly if the fabric is held slightly to the left as described. Continue to feed all pieces to be hemmed, in succession, without breaking machine thread. If it is necessary to cross seams, as on ruffles, cut a triangular snip from edges of seam to reduce bulk as it feeds. Do not pull fabric enough to cause seam to part.

**MACHINE HEMMER AS FOLDER**

For an even fold preparatory to making a small hand hem, run edges through hemmer without needle or thread.

**FALSE FRENCH SEAM**

On lightweight materials (e.g. percale or organdy), a nice seam, resembling a French seam, can be made in one stitching on the hemmer. Lay pieces to be seamed together, clip corners as for hem, and feed both edges through hemmer together. Pin edges at intervals so that one will not be pulled tighter than other.

### INSIDE-STITCHED TIE OR STRING

Join bias or straight strips to desired length. Fold wrong side out, lengthwise, and stitch. Do not close ends. To turn, attach safety pin to end and push through length. Be careful not to let material bunch too thickly. If pin comes loose, make small opening in seam and re-attach pin. Blind-stitch opening closed later.

### ATTACHING BIB TO WAISTBAND OR STRAP, BY INVISIBLE SEAM

*Fig. 1.* Make a crease in strap or waistband on its center fold line to serve as guide (shown by dot and dash line). Open flat again with right side up. C-D is inside of band or strap; E-F is outside. Lay bib A-B right side up on inside, parallel to crease but not quite covering it. Stitch ¼ inch from crease.

*Fig. 2.* Fold A-B over stitching line and stitch again, exactly on crease line of strap or waistband.

*Fig. 3.* Fold waistband or strap in usual manner. Fig. 3 shows belt folded on crease and bib attached invisibly.

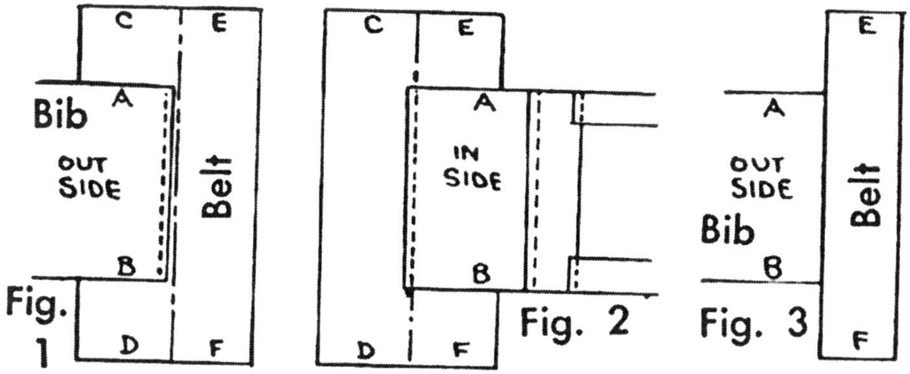


Fig. 1　Fig. 2　Fig. 3

### BIAS

A true bias is obtained by folding the lengthwise grain of the fabric at right angles to the crosswise grain and cutting on the resulting diagonal fold. Bias is more elastic than fabric cut on the straight of the goods, and therefore much used for facing or binding curves.

**Standard designations.** *Bias strip or facing* is fabric cut on the bias to any desired width, not folded (not sold commercially). *Single-fold bias tape* is bias strip with raw edges turned. Standard width, folded, is ½ inch. (This fits machine binder attachment.) *Double-fold bias tape* is bias strip with edges turned, then folded again in the center to form an edge binding. *Extra-width bias tape* is 1 inch wide after edges are turned.

### MAKING CONTINUOUS BIAS

If a quantity of bias is needed, mark strips on the true bias as shown, or if scissors guide is to be used, mark only strips A-B and C-D. Cut away triangles marked F (to make short strips later). Make a 2-inch cut along line between A and C (shown by dotted line). Skip end marked A and make a seam starting with end marked B, joining it to end marked C so that bias cutting lines meet at proposed stitching line ¼ inch from edge. Pin and stitch entire seam, forming a tube of fabric joined by spiral seam. Press seam open. Now, beginning at A, cut bias evenly in a continuous strip, ending at G.

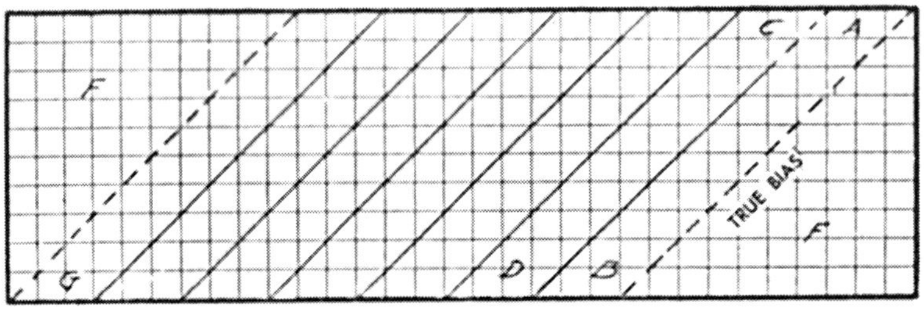


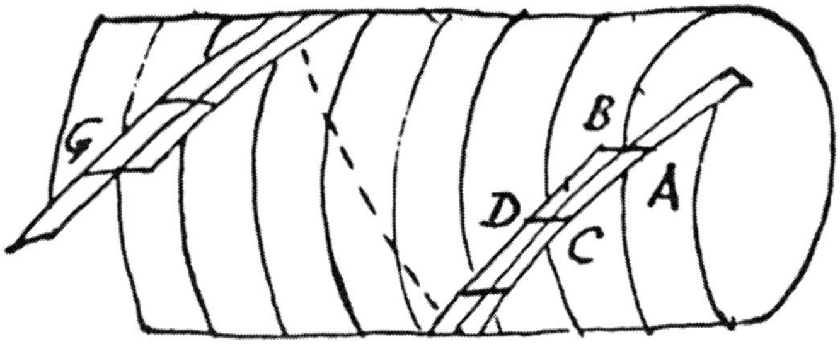

### USING SEWING MACHINE BINDER ATTACHMENT AS A FOLDER

Make continuous bias strip, as described, exactly 1 inch wide. Feed bias strip through folder and using medium hot iron, follow along just behind folder as it is drawn along length of bias. Wrap folded bias on a card.

### INVISIBLY STITCHED BIAS BINDING

Use double-fold bias tape. Notice that one folded edge extends slightly further than the other. Using the shorter edge, with right side of tape facing right side of fabric, open the fold and place raw edge of tape even with raw edge of fabric. Stitch exactly on crease of open fold. Trim seam if necessary. Fold other edge of tape over the fabric, keeping original fold. *From the right side,* stitch just inside bias binding but not on it, so that line of stitching falls right into joining line of first stitching. The underfold of tape should be caught by this stitching, which will be virtually invisible from the front. If stitching has skipped anywhere, whip down *by hand.*

### HANDLING PLASTIC MATERIAL

*Cutting.* Weight pattern down while cutting, or fasten with Scotch tape. *Do not pin.*

*Marking.* Make necessary marks with crayon or soft pencil.

*Joining.* Do not baste. Use paper clips, or pins lengthwise within seam allowance. Scotch tape may also be used.

*Stitching.* Use mercerized or nylon thread and make 8 stitches to the inch. Do not stitch too fast as plastic tends to creep. Raw edges, such as ruffles, need not be finished. Finish other edges with hems or bindings for strength.

# Apron Decorations

The possibilities for the decoration of aprons are so numerous that it will be possible only to suggest various types and give a few actual designs. (*Please note that the scale of these designs varies.* If not otherwise stated, each square equals 1 inch.) In addition to the designs shown, decorative motifs may be taken from other sources and scaled by means of marking the small drawing off in squares so that it may be enlarged just as the graphs in this book are meant to be done. A great variety of commercial transfers is also available.

**SPECIAL OCCASION DESIGNS**

*Valentine's Day.* Appliquéd pink and red hearts have blue ribbon embroidered in outline stitch entwined among them.

*Happy Birthday Party.* Chocolate colored false hem is accented with rickrack to simulate cake icing decorations, and "happy birthday" is written in small rickrack. Candles and flames are of appliqué.

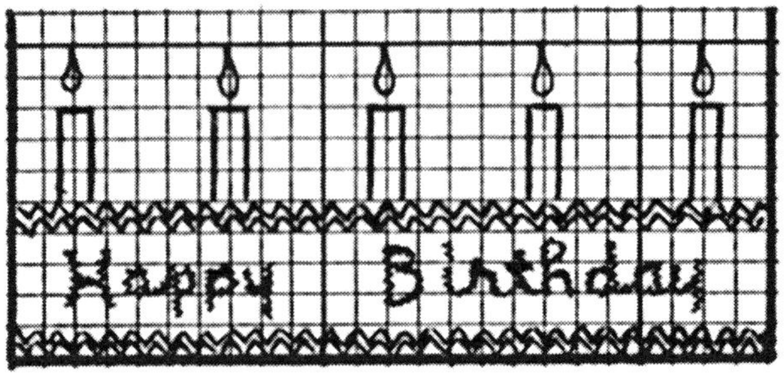

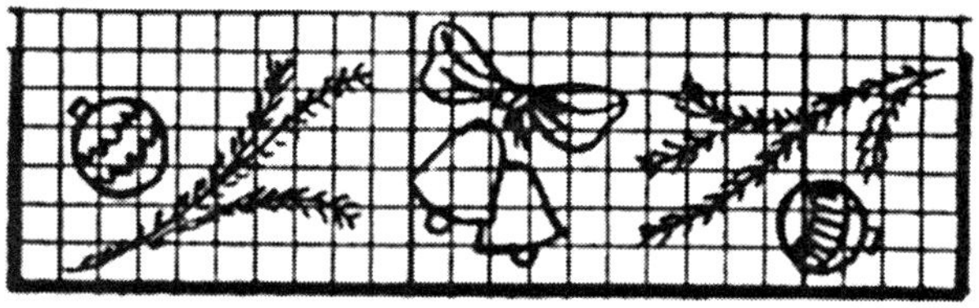

*Christmas.* Bells and bow are of appliqué with embroidery accents. Ornaments are of appliqué trimmed with embroidery stitches and rickrack. Pine sprigs are of outline stitch.

*Fourth of July.* Rockets are appliquéd in red and stars in white. Lines are of blue outline stitch. Border is red, white, and blue striped fabric. It also may be pieced together in these colors.

## SPECIAL OCCASION SUGGESTIONS

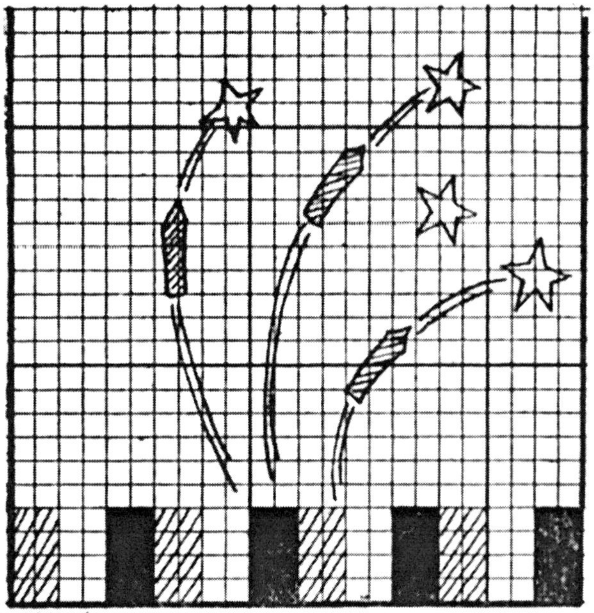

*Hallowe'en.* Fence is appliquéd in white, cat in black, and pumpkin in orange with outline stitch features. Add veins in brown.

# Appliqué

All appliqué designs are shown without seam allowance. They may be cut as shown, and the raw edges finished with buttonhole stitch worked close together. Or a ¼-inch seam allowance may be added, and turned in and the edges whipped down. Any additional lines such as veinings, should be embroidered in outline stitch. If desired, these same designs can be worked entirely in embroidery in suitable stitches.

BARBECUE DESIGN

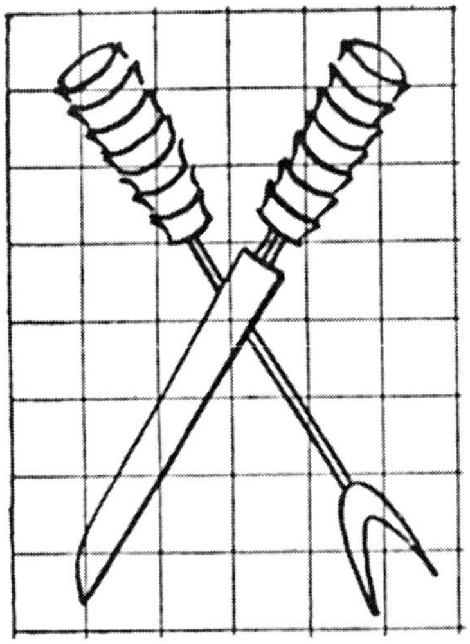

PENNSYLVANIA DUTCH

AMERICAN INDIAN DESIGNS

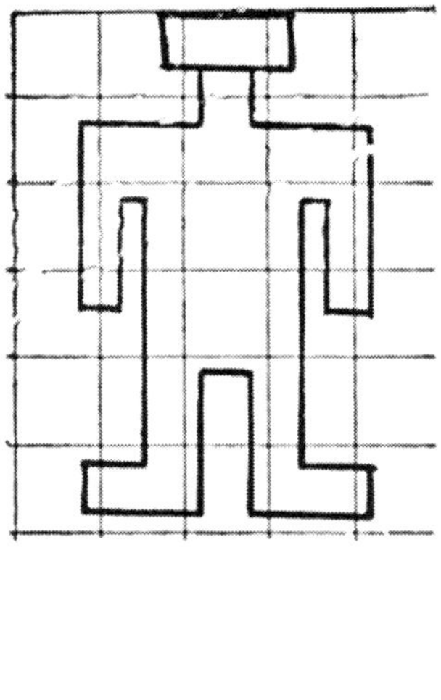

Buttonhole Stitch

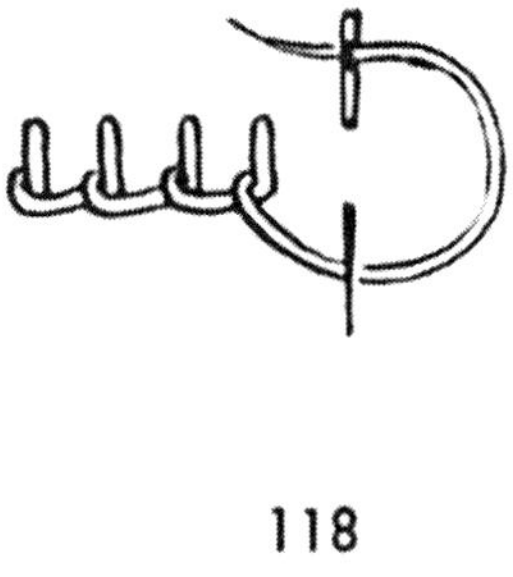

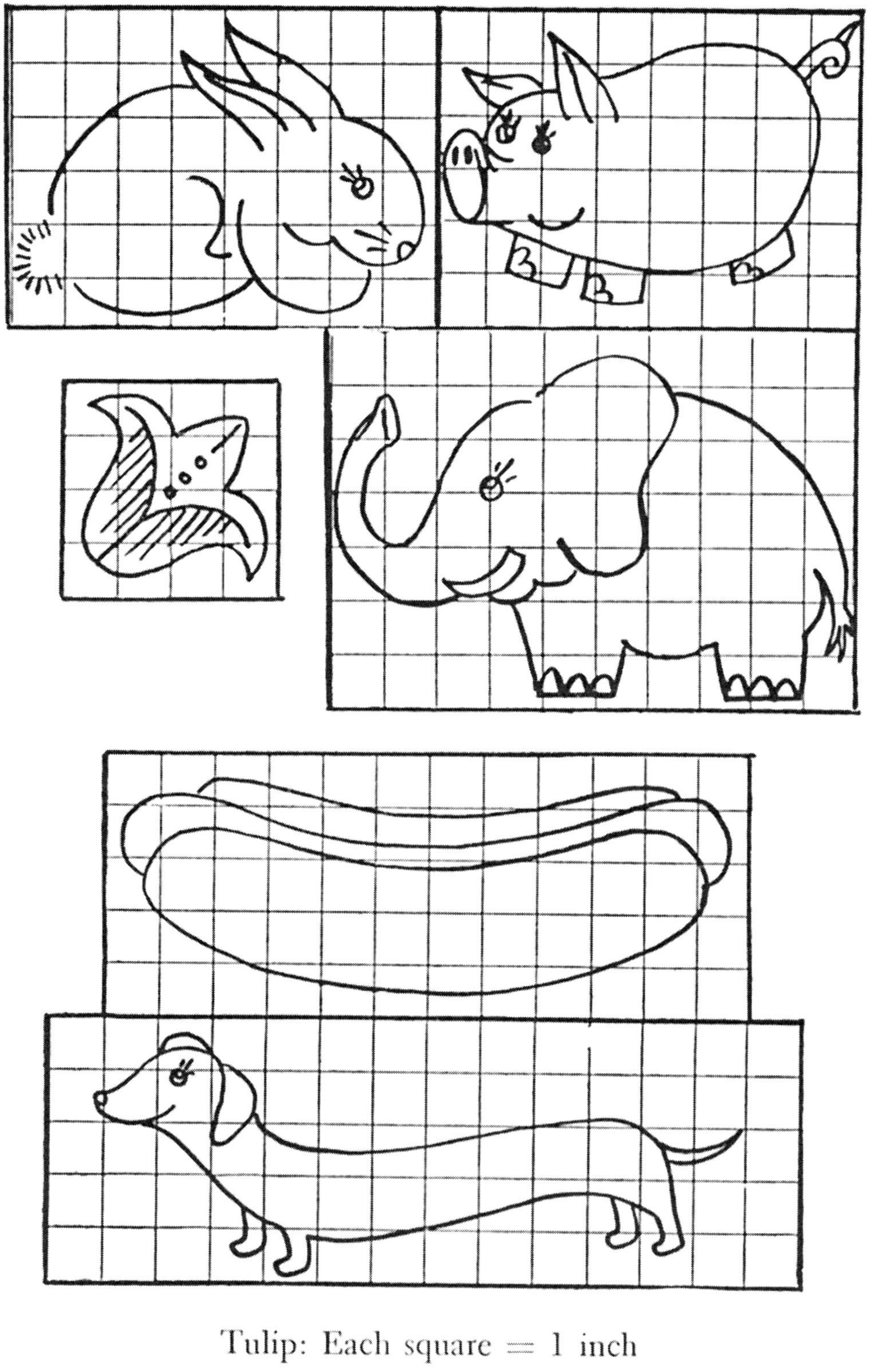

Tulip: Each square = 1 inch
Others: Each square = ½ inch

## Grape Cluster Appliqué Design

Arrangement of grape cluster and full-sized patterns of leaf and grape.

# Detached Appliqué

For these designs, each petal or wing is cut double (add ¼-inch seam allowance), stitched on heavy line, trimmed, and turned. They are then attached to apron by centers of flower or body of butterfly only. These may be appliquéd in usual manner or embroidered in satin stitch. Butterfly has two sets of wings, one larger than the other. Antennae are embroidered.

FULL-SIZE OUTLINES. INSERTS SHOW HOW PARTS ARE ASSEMBLED.

## Iron-on Appliqué

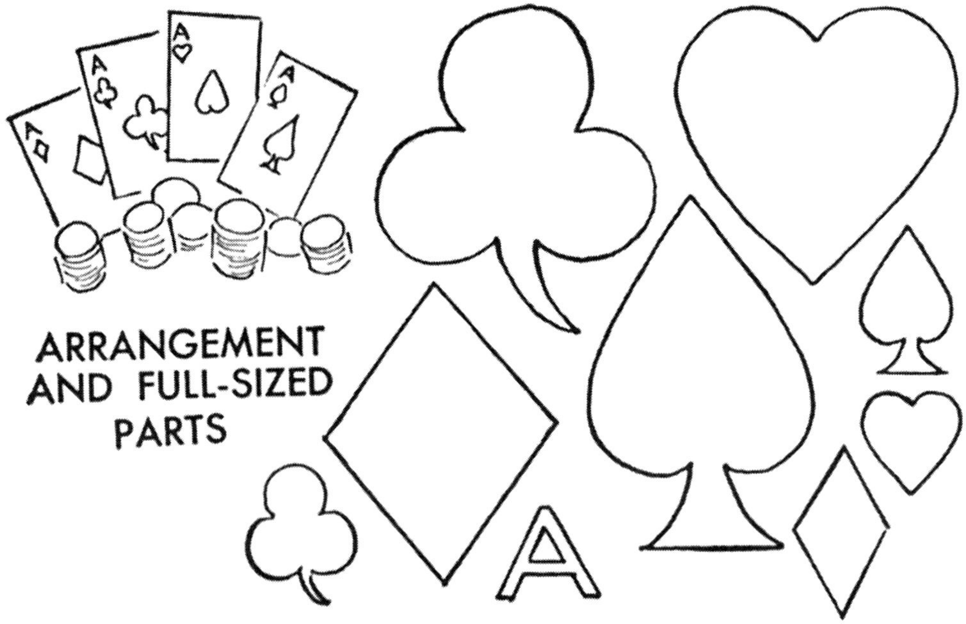


Quick appliqués can be made with the fabric sold as "iron-on" patches, available in a variety of colors and textures. First, make cut-out patterns of individual pieces of design. Group as closely as possible on "iron-on" fabric, draw around lightly with pencil, and cut on outline. Following directions on package, apply all parts of design to apron. *After all the parts have been ironed on,* add lines with sharpened crayon or a laundry-marking pen. Give a final pressing to set the markings, using a pressing cloth.

# Cross-Stitch

If tiny-squared dimity or gingham is used, fabric may be used as guide. Otherwise cross-stitch canvas must be used or the threads of the actual fabric counted.

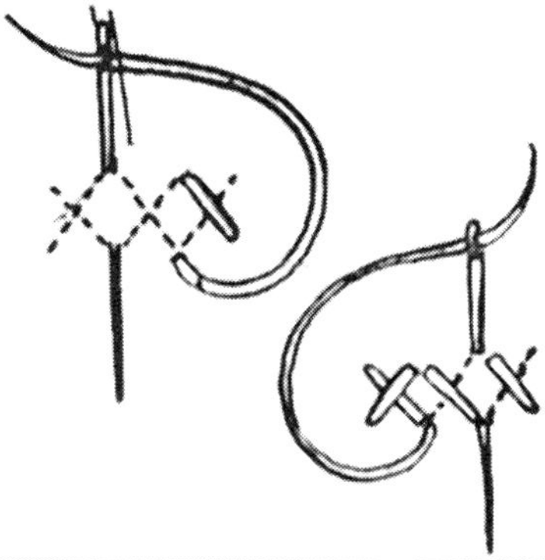

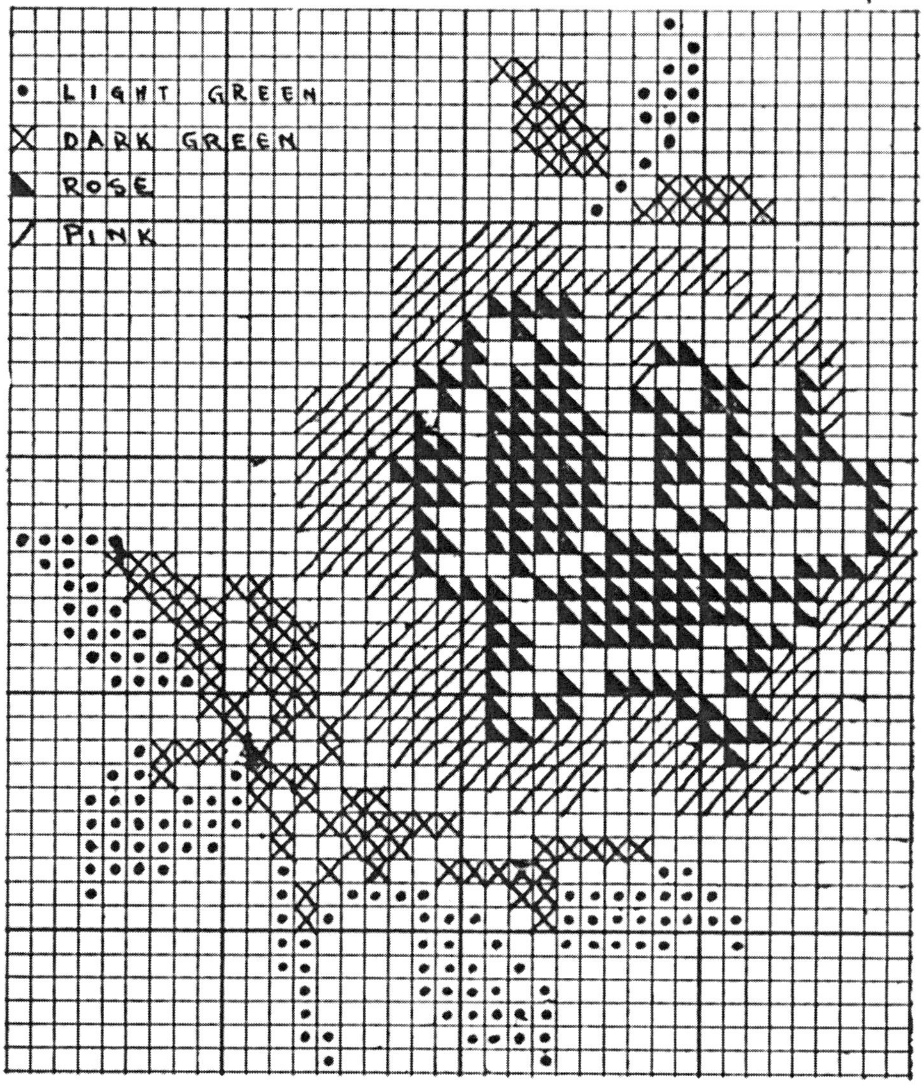

# Embroidery

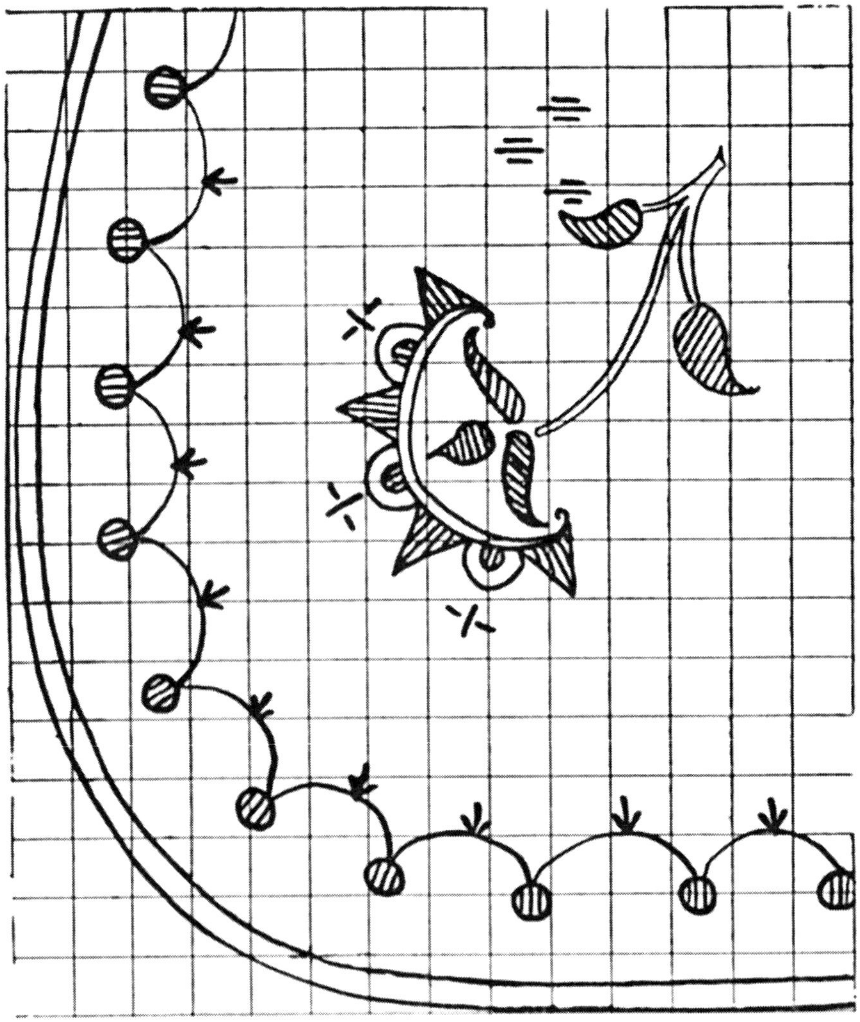

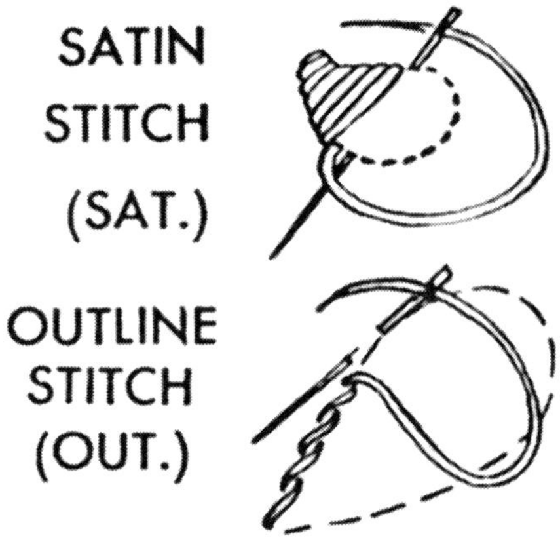


Circles, gold (g.) sat.; loops, green (gr.) out.; arrows, red (r.); stems, gr. out.; leaves, gr. sat.; center of flower, g. sat.; spine, r. out.; rounded petals, r. sat. with blue (bl.) sat. centers; pointed petals and crosses, bl.; lines above flower, r.

# Rickrack

If rickrack is to be stitched on by machine, take care not to apply it too tightly, as it shrinks when laundered and may pucker. This can be avoided by basting it first, being careful not to pull it. It can also be applied by hand with a few small stitches at each point. Or embroidery stitches such as those shown in Figs. 1 and 2 may be used for a more elegant effect. Fig. 3 shows two lengths of rickrack intertwined together. This should be applied by hand.

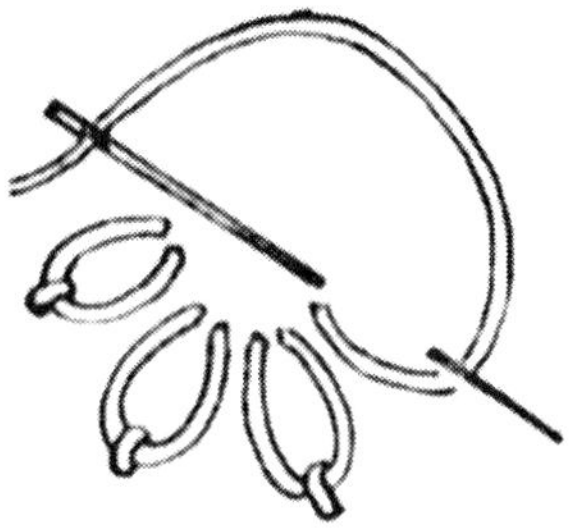

Stitch for Fig. 2

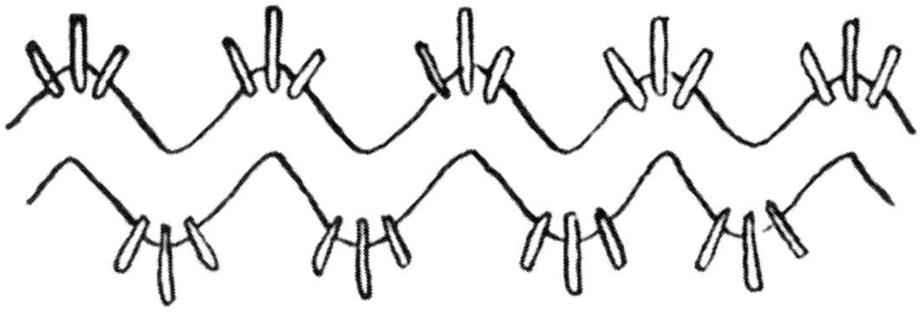

Fig. 1

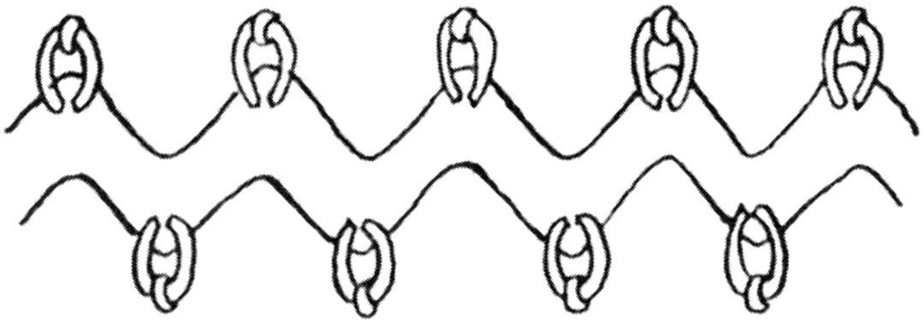

Fig. 2

Fig. 3

# Smocking

Prepare area to be smoked by marking with dots as shown in diagram below, or by using smocking transfer. For honeycomb smocking, the dots are drawn together in pairs as shown and each pair secured with two small stitches. Carrying thread between pairs underneath, work 2 rows at a time as shown by numbers. It is sometimes possible to use dotted, checked, or striped fabric as a guide instead of drawing the dots, if the spacing is right. For honeycomb smocking, the width of the fabric should be 2⅛ times the finished width desired.

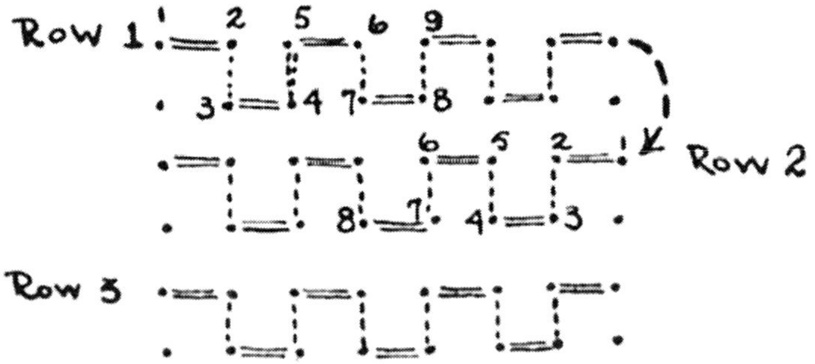


SMOCKING DIAGRAM

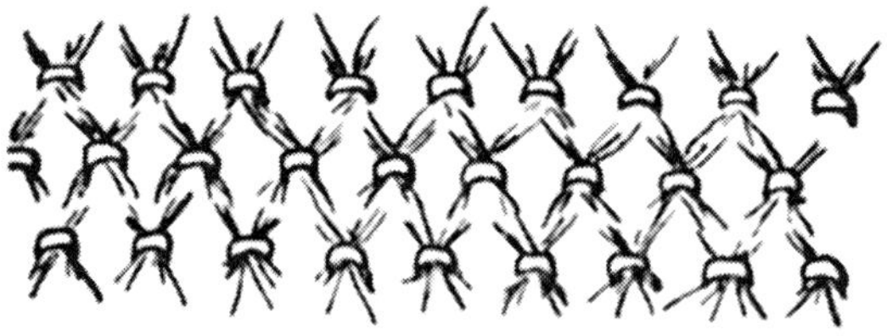

FINISHED SMOCKING

# Index

CPSIA information can be obtained at www.ICGtesting.com
Printed in the USA
LVOW121142140712

290076LV00001B/22/P